R Object-oriented Programming

A practical guide to help you learn and understand the programming techniques necessary to exploit the full power of R

Kelly Black

BIRMINGHAM - MUMBAI

R Object-oriented Programming

First published: October 2014

Production reference: 1201014

Published by Packt Publishing Ltd.
Livery Place
35 Livery Street
Birmingham B3 2PB, UK.

ISBN 978-1-78398-668-2

www.packtpub.com

Credits

Author
Kelly Black

Reviewers
Mzabalazo Z. Ngwenya
Prabhanjan Tattar
Tengfei Yin

Commissioning Editor
Akram Hussain

Acquisition Editor
Richard Brookes-Bland

Content Development Editor
Parita Khedekar

Technical Editor
Tanvi Bhatt

Copy Editors
Simran Bhogal
Sarang Chari
Ameesha Green
Paul Hindle
Karuna Narayanan

Project Coordinator
Neha Thakur

Proofreaders
Simran Bhogal
Maria Gould
Ameesha Green
Paul Hindle

Indexer
Priya Sane

Graphics
Disha Haria
Abhinash Sahu

Production Coordinator
Alwin Roy

Cover Work
Alwin Roy

About the Author

Kelly Black is a faculty member in the Department of Mathematics at Clarkson University. His background is in numerical analysis with a focus on the use of spectral methods and stochastic differential equations. He makes extensive use of R in the analysis of the results of Monte-Carlo simulations.

In addition to using R for his research interests, Kelly also uses the R environment for his statistics classes. He has extensive experience sharing his experiences with R in the classroom. The use of R to explore datasets is an important part of the curriculum.

I would like to thank my wife and daughter for their support and inspiration. You are my life, and we do this together.

I also wish to thank to thank the people who took a direct role in bringing this book to completion. In particular, thanks go to the Content Development Editor, Parita Khedekar, for her work in assembling everything, keeping me on track, and ensuring the overall integrity of this book. Additional thanks go to the Technical Editor, Tanvi Bhatt, for maintaining the integrity of the book as a whole and, technical guidance. Thank you!

I would also like to thank the reviewers. Unfortunately, some of your insights were not able to be integrated into this work. I did read your reviews and valued them. I tried to balance your concerns to the best of my ability. Thank you as well.

About the Reviewers

Mzabalazo Z. Ngwenya has worked extensively in the field of statistical consulting and currently works as a biometrician. He has an MSc in Mathematical Statistics from the University of Cape Town and is presently studying for a PhD. His research interests include statistical computing, machine learning, and spatial statistics. Previously, he was involved in reviewing Packt Publishing's *Learning RStudio for R Statistical Computing*, *R Statistical Application Development by Example Beginner's Guide*, and *Machine Learning with R*.

Prabhanjan Tattar is currently working as a Business Analysis Senior Advisor at Dell Global Analytics, Dell. He has 7 years of experience as a statistical analyst. Survival analysis and statistical inference are his main areas of research/interest, and he has published several research papers in peer-reviewed journals and also authored two books on R: *R Statistical Application Development by Example*, Packt Publishing, and *A Course in Statistics with R*, Narosa Publishing. The R packages, gpk and RSADBE are also maintained by him.

Tengfei Yin earned his PhD in Molecular, Cellular, and Developmental Biology (MCDB) with a focus on computational biology and bioinformatics from Iowa State University, with a minor in Statistics. His research interests include information visualization, high-throughput biological data analysis, data mining, and applied statistical genetics. He has developed and maintained several software packages in R and Bioconductor.

www.PacktPub.com

Support files, eBooks, discount offers, and more

You might want to visit www.PacktPub.com for support files and downloads related to your book.

Did you know that Packt offers eBook versions of every book published, with PDF and ePub files available? You can upgrade to the eBook version at www.PacktPub. com and as a print book customer, you are entitled to a discount on the eBook copy. Get in touch with us at service@packtpub.com for more details.

At www.PacktPub.com, you can also read a collection of free technical articles, sign up for a range of free newsletters and receive exclusive discounts and offers on Packt books and eBooks.

http://PacktLib.PacktPub.com

Do you need instant solutions to your IT questions? PacktLib is Packt's online digital book library. Here, you can access, read and search across Packt's entire library of books.

Why subscribe?

- Fully searchable across every book published by Packt
- Copy and paste, print and bookmark content
- On demand and accessible via web browser

Free access for Packt account holders

If you have an account with Packt at www.PacktPub.com, you can use this to access PacktLib today and view nine entirely free books. Simply use your login credentials for immediate access.

Table of Contents

Preface

The R environment is a powerful software suite that started as a model for the S language originally developed at Bell Laboratories. The original code base was created by Ross Ihaka and Robert Gentleman in 1993. It rapidly grew with the help of others, and it has since become a standard in statistical computing. The software suite itself has grown well beyond an implementation of a language and has become an "environment". It is extensible, and the wide variety of packages that are available help make it a powerful resource that continues to grow in popularity and power.

Our aim in this book is to provide a resource for programming using the R language, and we assume that you will be making use of the R environment to implement and test your code. The book can be roughly divided into four parts. In the first part, we provide a discussion of the basic ideas and topics necessary to understand how R classifies data and the options that can be used to make calculations from data. In the second part, we provide a discussion of how R organizes data and the options available to keep track of data, display data, and read and save data. In the third part, we provide a discussion on programming topics specific to the R language and the options available for object-oriented programming. In the fourth part, we provide several extended examples as a way to demonstrate how all of the topics can fit together to solve problems.

What this book covers

A list of the chapters is given here. The first three chapters focus on the basic requirements associated with getting data into the system and the most basic tasks associated with calculations associated with data. The next three chapters focus on the miscellaneous issues that arise in practice when working with and examining data including the mechanics of dealing with different data types. The next three chapters focus on basic and advanced programming topics. The final three chapters provide more detailed examples to demonstrate how all of the ideas can be brought together to solve problems.

Chapter 1, Data Types, offers a broad overview of the different data types. This includes basic representations such as float, double, complex, factors, and integer representations, and it also includes examples of how to enter vectors through the interactive shell. A brief discussion of the most basic operations and how to interact with the R shell is also given.

Chapter 2, Organizing Data, offers a more detailed look at the way data is organized within the R environment. Additional topics include how to access the data as well as how to perform basic operations on the various data structures. The primary data structures examined are lists, arrays, tables, and data frames.

Chapter 3, Saving Data and Printing Results, offers a detailed look at the ways to bring data into the R environment and builds on the topics discussed in the previous chapter. Additional topics revolve around the ways to display results as well as various ways to save data.

Chapter 4, Calculating Probabilities and Random Numbers, offers a detailed examination of the probability and sampling features of the R language. The R environment includes a number of features to aid in the way data can be analyzed. Any statistical analysis includes an underlying reliance on probability, and it is a topic that cannot be ignored. The availability of a wide variety of probability and sampling options is one of the strengths of the R language, and we explore some of the options in this chapter.

Chapter 5, Character and String Operations, offers a detailed examination of the various options available for examining, testing, and performing operations on strings. This is an important topic because it is not uncommon for datasets to have inconsistencies, and a routine that reads data from a file should include some basic checks.

Chapter 6, Converting and Defining Time Variables, offers a detailed examination of the time data structure. A basic introduction is given in the first chapter, and more details are provided in this chapter. The prevalence of time-related data makes the topic of these data structures too important to ignore.

Chapter 7, Basic Programming, offers a detailed examination of the most basic flow controls and programming features of the R language. The chapter provides details about conditional execution as well as the various looping constructs. Additionally, mundane topics associated with writing programs, execution, and formatting are also discussed.

Chapter 8, S3 Classes, offers a detailed examination of S3 classes. This is the first and most common approach to object-oriented programming. The use of S3 classes can be confusing to people already familiar with object-oriented programming, but their flexibility has made them a popular way to approach object-oriented programming in R.

Chapter 9, S4 Classes, offers a detailed examination of S4 classes. This is a more recent approach to object-oriented programming compared to S3 classes. It is a more structured approach and is more familiar to people who have experience with object-oriented programming.

Chapter 10, Case Study – Course Grades, offers an in-depth example of a grade-tracking application. This is the first of three examples, and it is the simplest example. It was chosen as it is something that is likely to be more familiar to a wider range of people.

Chapter 11, Case Study – Simulation, offers an in-depth example of an application that is used to generate data based on Monte-Carlo simulations. The application demonstrates how an object-oriented approach can be used to create an environment used to execute simulations, organize the results, and perform a basic analysis on the results.

Chapter 12, Case Study – Regression, offers an in-depth example of an application that offers a wide range of options you can use to perform regression. Regression is a common task and occurs in a wide variety of contexts. The application that is developed demonstrates a flexible way to handle both continuous and ordinal data as a way to demonstrate the use of a flexible object-oriented approach. You can download this chapter form `https://www.packtpub.com/sites/default/files/downloads/6682OS_Case_Study_Regression.pdf`.

Appendix, Package Management, gives a brief overview of installing, updating, and removing packages is given. Packages are libraries that can be added to R that extend its capabilities. Being able to extend R and make use of other libraries represents one R's more powerful features.

What you need for this book

It is assumed that you will be working in the R environment, and the example code has been developed and tested for R version 3.0.1 and later. The R environment is a type of free software and is made available through the efforts and generosity of the R Foundation. It can be downloaded from http://www.r-project.org/. The material in the first half of the book assumes that you have access to R and can work from the interactive command line within the R environment. The material in the second half of the book assumes that you are familiar with programming and can write and save computer code. At a minimum, you should have access to a programming editor and should be familiar with directory structures and search paths.

Who this book is for

If you are familiar with programming and wish to gain a basic understanding of the R environment and learn how to create programming applications using the R language, this is the book for you. It is assumed that you have some exposure to the R environment and have a basic understanding of R. This book does not provide extensive motivations for certain approaches and practices assuming that the reader is comfortable in the development of software applications.

Conventions

In this book, you will find a number of styles of text that distinguish between different kinds of information. Here are some examples of these styles, and an explanation of their meaning.

Code words in text, database table names, folder names, filenames, file extensions, pathnames, dummy URLs, user input, and Twitter handles are shown as follows: "A list is created using the `list` command, and a variable can be tested or coerced using the `is.list` and `as.list` commands."

A block of code is set as follows:

```
> x = rnorm(5,mean=10,sd=3)
> x
[1] 11.172719  8.784284 10.074035  5.735171 10.800138
> pnorm(abs(x-10),mean=0,sd=3)-pnorm(-abs(x-10),mean=0,sd=3)
[1] 0.30413363 0.31469803 0.01968849 0.84486037 0.21030971
>
```

When we wish to draw your attention to a particular part of a code block, the relevant lines or items are set in bold:

```
> v <- c(1,3,5,7,-10)
> v
[1]    1   3    5    7 -10
> v[4]
[1]  7
> v[2] <- v[1]-v[5]
> v
[1]    1  11    5    7 -10
```

New terms and **important words** are shown in bold.

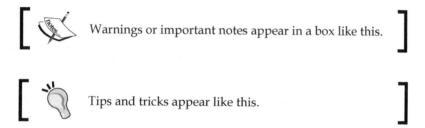

Warnings or important notes appear in a box like this.

Tips and tricks appear like this.

Reader feedback

Feedback from our readers is always welcome. Let us know what you think about this book—what you liked or may have disliked. Reader feedback is important for us to develop titles that you really get the most out of.

To send us general feedback, simply send an e-mail to feedback@packtpub.com, and mention the book title via the subject of your message.

If there is a topic that you have expertise in and you are interested in either writing or contributing to a book, see our author guide on www.packtpub.com/authors.

Customer support

Now that you are the proud owner of a Packt book, we have a number of things to help you to get the most from your purchase.

Downloading the example code

You can download the example code files for all Packt books you have purchased from your account at http://www.packtpub.com. An additional source for the examples in this book can be found at https://github.com/KellyBlack/R-Object-Oriented-Programming. If you purchased this book elsewhere, you can visit http://www.packtpub.com/support and register to have the files e-mailed directly to you.

Errata

Although we have taken every care to ensure the accuracy of our content, mistakes do happen. If you find a mistake in one of our books—maybe a mistake in the text or the code—we would be grateful if you would report this to us. By doing so, you can save other readers from frustration and help us improve subsequent versions of this book. If you find any errata, please report them by visiting http://www.packtpub.com/submit-errata, selecting your book, clicking on the **errata submission form** link, and entering the details of your errata. Once your errata are verified, your submission will be accepted and the errata will be uploaded on our website, or added to any list of existing errata, under the Errata section of that title. Any existing errata can be viewed by selecting your title from http://www.packtpub.com/support.

Copyright violations

Violation of copyright laws for material on the Internet is an ongoing problem across all media. At Packt, we take the protection of our copyright and licenses very seriously. If you come across any illegal copies of our works, in any form, on the Internet, please provide us with the location address or website name immediately so that we can pursue a remedy.

Please contact us at copyright@packtpub.com with a link to the suspected pirated material.

We appreciate your help in protecting our authors, and our ability to bring you valuable content.

Questions

You can contact us at questions@packtpub.com if you are having a problem with any aspect of the book, and we will do our best to address it.

1

Data Types

In this chapter, we provide a broad overview of the different data types available in the R environment. This material is introductory in nature, and this chapter ensures that important information on implementing algorithms is available to you. There are roughly five parts in this chapter:

- **Working with variables in the R environment**: This section gives you a broad overview of interacting with the R shell, creating variables, deleting variables, saving variables, and loading variables

- **Discrete data types**: This section gives you an overview of the principle data types used to represent discrete data

- **Continuous data types**: This section gives you an overview of the principle data types used to represent continuous data

- **Introduction to vectors**: This section gives you an introduction to vectors and manipulating vectors in R

- **Special data types**: This section gives you a list of other data types that do not fit in the other categories or have other meanings

Assignment

The R environment is an interactive shell. Commands are entered using the keyboard, and the environment should feel familiar to anyone used to MATLAB or the Python interactive interpreter. To assign a value to a variable, you can usually use the = symbol in the same way as these other interpreters. The difference with R, however, is that there are other ways to assign a variable, and their behavior depends on the context.

Another way to assign a value to a variable is to use the <- symbols (sometimes called operators). At first glance, it seems odd to have different ways to assign a value, but we will see that variables can be saved in different environments. The same name may be used in different environments, and the name can be ambiguous. We will adopt the use of the <- operator in this text because it is the most common operator, and it is also the least likely to cause confusion in different contexts.

The R environment manages memory and variable names dynamically. To create a new variable, simply assign a value to it, as follows:

```
> a <- 6
> a
[1] 6
```

A variable has a scope, and the meaning of a variable name can vary depending on the context. For example, if you refer to a variable within a function (think subroutine) or after attaching a dataset, then there may be multiple variables in the workspace with the same name. The R environment maintains a search path to determine which variable to use, and we will discuss these details as they arise.

The <- operator for the assignment will work in any context while the = operator only works for complete expressions. Another option is to use the <<- operator. The advantage of the <<- operator is that it instructs the R environment to search parent environments to see whether the variable already exists. In some contexts, within a function for example, the <- operator will create a new variable; however, the <<- operator will make use of an existing variable outside of the function if it is found.

Another way to assign variables is to use the -> and ->> operators. These operators are similar to those given previously. The only difference is that they reverse the direction of assignment, as follows:

```
> 14.5 -> a
> 1/12.0 ->> b
> a
[1] 14.5
> b
[1] 0.08333333
```

The workspace

The R environment keeps track of variables as well as allocates and manages memory as it is requested. One command to list the currently defined variables is the ls command. A variable can be deleted using the rm command. In the following example, the a and b variables have been changed, and the a variable is deleted:

```
> a <-  17.5
> b <-  99/4
> ls()
[1] "a" "b"
> objects()
[1] "a" "b"
> rm(a)
> ls()
[1]  "b"
```

If you wish to delete all of the variables in the workspace, the list option in the rm command can be combined with the ls command, as follows:

```
> ls()
[1] "b"
> rm(list=ls())
> ls()
character(0)
```

A wide variety of other options are available. For example, there are directory options to show and set the current directory, as follows:

```
> getwd()
[1]  "/home/black"
> setwd("/tmp")
> getwd()
[1]  "/tmp"
> dir()
 [1]  "antActivity.R"           "betterS3.R"
 [3]  "chiSquaredArea.R"        "firstS3.R"
 [5]  "math100.csv"             "opsTesting.R"
 [7]  "probabilityExampleOne.png" "s3.R"
 [9]  "s4Example.R"
```

Another important task is to save and load a workspace. The `save` and `save.image` commands can be used to save the current workspace. The `save` command allows you to save a particular variable, and the `save.image` command allows you to save the entire workspace. The usage of these commands is as follows:

```
> save(a,file="a.RData")
> save.image("wholeworkspace.Rdata")
```

These commands have a variety of options. For example, the `ascii` option is a commonly used option to ensure that the data file is in a (nearly) human-readable form. The `help` command can be used to get more details and see more of the options that are available. In the following example, the variable `a` is saved in a file, `a.RData`, and the file is saved in a human-readable format:

```
> save(a,file="a.RData",ascii=TRUE)
> save.image(" wholeworkspace.RData",ascii=TRUE)
> help(save)
```

As an alternative to the `help` command, the `?` operator can also be used to get the help page for a given command. An additional command is the `help.search` command that is used to search the help files for a given string. The `??` operator is also available to perform a search for a given string.

The information in a file can be read back into the workspace using the `load` command:

```
> load("a.RData")
> ls()
[1] "a"
> a
[1] 19
```

Another question that arises with respect to a variable is how it is stored. The two commands to determine this are `mode` and `storage.mode`. You should try to use these commands for each of the data types described in the following subsections. Basically, these commands can make it easier to determine whether a variable is a numeric value or another basic data type.

The previous commands provide options for saving the values of the variables within a workspace. They do not save the commands that you have entered. These commands are referred to as the history within the R workspace, and you can save your history using the `savehistory` command. The history can be displayed using the `history` command, and the `loadhistory` command can be used to replay the commands in a file.

The last command given here is the command to quit, q(). Some people consider this to be the most important command because without it you would never be able to leave R. The rest of us are not sure why it is necessary.

Discrete data types

One of the features of the R environment is the rich collection of data types that are available. Here, we briefly list some of the built-in data types that describe discrete data. The four data types discussed are the integer, logical, character, and factor data types. We also introduce the idea of a vector, which is the default data structure for any variable. A list of the commands discussed here is given in *Table 2* and *Table 3*.

It should be noted that the default data type in R, for a number, is a double precision number. Strings can be interpreted in a variety of ways, usually as either a string or a factor. You should be careful to make sure that R is storing information in the format that you want, and it is important to double-check this important aspect of how data is tracked.

Integer

The first discrete data type examined is the integer type. Values are 32-bit integers. In most circumstances, a number must be explicitly cast as being an integer, as the default type in R is a double precision number. There are a variety of commands used to cast integers as well as allocate space for integers. The integer command takes a number for an argument and will return a vector of integers whose length is given by the argument:

```
> bubba <- integer(12)
> bubba
 [1] 0 0 0 0 0 0 0 0 0 0 0 0
> bubba[1]
[1] 0
> bubba[2]
[1] 0
> bubba[[4]]
[1] 0
>  b[4] <- 15
> b
 [1]  0  0  0 15  0  0  0  0  0  0  0  0
```

In the preceding example, a vector of twelve integers was defined. The default values are zero, and the individual entries in the vector are accessed using braces. The first entry in the vector has index 1, so in this example, bubba [1] refers to the initial entry in the vector. Note that there are two ways to access an element in the vector: single versus double braces. For a vector, the two methods are nearly the same, but when we explore the use of lists as opposed to vectors, the meaning will change. In short, the double braces return objects of the same type as the elements within the vector, and the single braces return values of the same type as the variable itself. For example, using single braces on a list will return a list, while double braces may return a vector.

A number can be cast as an integer using the as.integer command. A variable's type can be checked using the typeof command. The typeof command indicates how R stores the object and is different from the class command, which is an attribute that you can change or query:

```
> as.integer(13.2)
[1] 13
> thisNumber <- as.integer(8/3)
> typeof(thisNumber)
[1] "integer"
```

Note that a sequence of numbers can be automatically created using either the : operator or the seq command:

```
> 1:5
[1] 1 2 3 4 5
> myNum <- as.integer(1:5)


> myNum[1]
[1] 1
> myNum[3]
[1] 3

> seq(4,11,by=2)
[1]   4   6   8  10
> otherNums <- seq(4,11,by=2)


> otherNums[3]
[1] 8
```

A common task is to determine whether or not a variable is of a certain type. For integers, the `is.integer` command is used to determine whether or not a variable has an integer type:

```
> a <- 1.2
> typeof(a)
[1] "double"
> is.integer(a)
[1] FALSE
> a <- as.integer(1.2)
> typeof(a)
[1] "integer"
> is.integer(a)
[1] TRUE
```

Logical

Logical data consists of variables that are either true or false. The words TRUE and FALSE are used to designate the two possible values of a logical variable. (The TRUE value can also be abbreviated to T, and the FALSE value can be abbreviated to F.) The basic commands associated with logical variables are similar to the commands for integers discussed in the previous subsection. The `logical` command is used to allocate a vector of Boolean values. In the following example, a logical vector of length 10 is created. The default value is FALSE, and the Boolean *not* operator is used to flip the values to evaluate to TRUE:

```
> b <- logical(10)
> b
 [1] FALSE FALSE FALSE FALSE FALSE FALSE FALSE FALSE FALSE FALSE
> b[3]
[1] FALSE
> !b
 [1] TRUE TRUE TRUE TRUE TRUE TRUE TRUE TRUE TRUE TRUE
> !b[5]
[1] TRUE
> typeof(b)
[1] "logical"
> mode(b)
[1] "logical"
> storage.mode(b)
[1] "logical"
>  b[3] <- TRUE
> b
 [1] FALSE FALSE  TRUE FALSE FALSE FALSE FALSE FALSE FALSE FALSE
```

To cast a value to a logical type, you can use the `as.logical` command. Note that zero is mapped to a value of FALSE and other numbers are mapped to a value of TRUE:

```
> a <- -1:1
> a
[1] -1  0  1
> as.logical(a)
[1]   TRUE FALSE   TRUE
```

To determine whether or not a value has a logical type, you use the `is.logical` command:

```
> b <- logical(4)
> b
[1] FALSE FALSE FALSE FALSE
> is.logical(b)
[1] TRUE
```

The standard operators for logical operations are available, and a list of some of the more common operations is given in *Table 1*. Note that there is a difference between operations such as & and &&. A single & is used to perform an and operation on each pairwise element of two vectors, while the double && returns a single logical result using only the first elements of the vectors:

```
> l1 <- c(TRUE,FALSE)
> l2 <- c(TRUE,TRUE)
> l1&l1
[1]   TRUE FALSE
> l1&&l1
[1] TRUE
> l1|l2
[1] TRUE TRUE
> l1||l2
[1] TRUE
```

You can download the example code files for all Packt books you have purchased from your account at http://www.packtpub.com. An additional source for the examples in this book can be found at https://github.com/KellyBlack/R-Object-Oriented-Programming. If you purchased this book elsewhere, you can visit http://www.packtpub.com/support and register to have the files e-mailed directly to you.

The following table shows various logical operators and their description:

Logical Operator	Description
<	Less than
>	Greater that
<=	Less than or equal to
>=	Greater than or equal to
==	Equal to
!=	Not equal to
|	Entrywise or
||	Or
!	Not
&	Entrywise and
&&	And
xor(a,b)	Exclusive or

Table 1 – list of operators for logical variables

Character

One common way to store information is to save data as characters or strings. Character data is defined using either single or double quotes:

```
> a <- "hello"
> a
[1] "hello"
> b <- 'there'
> b
[1] "there"
> typeof(a)
[1] "character"
```

The character command can be used to allocate a vector of character-valued strings, as follows:

```
> many <- character(3)
> many
[1] "" "" ""
> many[2] <- "this is the second"
> many[3] <- 'yo, third!'
> many[1] <- "and the first"
> many
[1] "and the first"      "this is the second" "yo, third!"
```

A value can be cast as a character using the `as.character` command, as follows:

```
> a <- 3.0
> a
[1] 3
> b <- as.character(a)
> b
[1] "3"
```

Finally, the `is.character` command takes a single argument, and it returns a value of TRUE if the argument is a string:

```
> a <- as.character(4.5)
> a
[1] "4.5"
> is.character(a)
[1] TRUE
```

Factors

Another common way to record data is to provide a discrete set of levels. For example, the results of an individual trial in an experiment may be denoted by a value of a, b, or c. Ordinal data of this kind is referred to as a factor in R. The commands and ideas are roughly parallel to the data types described previously. There are some subtle differences with factors, though. Factors are used to designate different levels and can be considered ordered or unordered. There are a large number of options, and it is wise to consult the help pages for factors using the `(help(factor))` command. One thing to note, though, is that the `typeof` command for a factor will return an integer.

Factors can be defined using the `factor` command, as follows:

```
> lev <- factor(x=c("one","two","three","one"))
> lev
[1] one    two    three one
Levels: one three two
> levels(lev)
[1] "one"   "three" "two"
> sort(lev)
[1] one    one    two    three
Levels: one two three

> lev <- factor(x=c("one","two","three","one"),levels=c("one","two",
"three"))
> lev
```

```
[1] one     two     three one
Levels: one two three
> levels(lev)
[1] "one"    "two"    "three"
> sort(lev)
[1] one     one     two     three
Levels: one two three
```

The techniques used to cast a variable to a factor or test whether a variable is a factor are similar to the previous examples. A variable can be cast as a factor using the as.factor command. Also, the is.factor command can be used to determine whether or not a variable has a type of factor.

Continuous data types

The data types for continuous data types are given here. The double and complex data types are given. A list of the commands discussed here is given in *Table 2* and *Table 3*.

Double

The default numeric data type in R is a double precision number. The commands are similar to those of the integer data type discussed previously. The double command can be used to allocate a vector of double precision numbers, and the numbers within the vector are accessed using braces:

```
> d <- double(8)
> d
[1] 0 0 0 0 0 0 0 0
> typeof(d)
[1] "double"
> d[3] <- 17
> d
[1]  0  0 17  0  0  0  0  0
```

The techniques used to cast a variable to a double precision number and test whether a variable is a double precision number are similar to the examples seen previously. A variable can be cast as a double precision number using the as.double command. Also, to determine whether a variable is a double precision number, the as.double command can be used.

Complex

Arithmetic for complex numbers is supported in R, and most math functions will react properly when given a complex number. You can append i to the end of a number to force it to be the imaginary part of a complex number, as follows:

```
> 1i
[1] 0+1i
> 1i*1i
[1] -1+0i
> z <- 3+2i
> z
[1] 3+2i
> z*z
[1] 5+12i
> Mod(z)
[1] 3.605551
> Re(z)
[1] 3
> Im(z)
[1] 2
> Arg(z)
[1] 0.5880026
> Conj(z)
[1] 3-2i
```

The complex command can also be used to define a vector of complex numbers. There are a number of options for the complex command, so a quick check of the help page, (help(complex)), is recommended:

```
> z <- complex(3)
> z
[1] 0+0i 0+0i 0+0i
> typeof(z)
[1] "complex"
> z <- complex(real=c(1,2),imag=c(3,4))
> z
[1] 1+3i 2+4i
> Re(z)
[1] 1 2
```

The techniques to cast a variable to a complex number and to test whether or not a variable is a complex number are similar to the methods seen previously. A variable can be cast as complex using the as.complex command. Also, to test whether or not a variable is a complex number, the as.complex command can be used.

Special data types

There are two other common data types that occur that are important. We will discuss these two data types and provide a note about objects. The two data types are NA and NULL. These are brief comments, as these are recurring topics that we will revisit many times.

The first data type is a constant, NA. This is a type used to indicate a missing value. It is a constant in R, and a variable can be tested using the is.na command, as follows:

```
> n <- c(NA,2,3,NA,5)
> n
[1] NA  2  3 NA  5
> is.na(n)
[1]  TRUE FALSE FALSE  TRUE FALSE
> n[!is.na(n)]
[1] 2 3 5
```

Another special type is the NULL type. It has the same meaning as the null keyword in the C language. It is not an actual type but is used to determine whether or not an object exists:

```
> a <- NULL
> typeof(a)
[1] "NULL"
```

Finally, we'll quickly explore the term objects. The variables that we defined in all of the preceding examples are treated as objects within the R environment. When we start writing functions and creating classes, it will be important to realize that they are treated like variables. The names used to assign variables are just a shortcut for R to determine where an object is located.

For example, the complex command is used to allocate a vector of complex values. The command is defined to be a set of instructions, and there is an object called complex that points to those instructions:

```
> complex
function (length.out = 0L, real = numeric(), imaginary = numeric(),
    modulus = 1, argument = 0)
{
    if (missing(modulus) && missing(argument)) {
        .Internal(complex(length.out, real, imaginary))
    }
    else {
        n <- max(length.out, length(argument), length(modulus))
```

```
        rep_len(modulus, n)  * exp((0+1i)  * rep_len(argument,
            n))
    }
}
<bytecode: 0x2489c80>
<environment: namespace:base>
```

There is a difference between calling the `complex()` function and referring to the set of instructions located at `complex`.

Notes on the as and is functions

Two common tasks are to determine whether a variable is of a given type and to cast a variable to different types. The commands to determine whether a variable is of a given type generally start with the `is` prefix, and the commands to cast a variable to a different type generally start with the `as` prefix. The list of commands to determine whether a variable is of a given type are given in the following table:

Type to check	Command
Integer	`is.integer`
Logical	`is.logical`
Character	`is.character`
Factor	`is.factor`
Double	`is.double`
Complex	`is.complex`
NA	`is.NA`
List	`is.list`

Table 2 – commands to determine whether a variable is of a particular type

The commands used to cast a variable to a different type are given in *Table 3*. These commands take a single argument and return a variable of the given type. For example, the `as.character` command can be used to convert a number to a string.

The commands in the previous table are used to test what type a variable has. The following table provides the commands that are used to change a variable of one type to another type:

Type to convert to	Command
Integer	as.integer
Logical	as.logical
Character	as.character
Factor	as.factor
Double	as.double
Complex	as.complex
NA	as.NA
List	as.list

Table 3 – commands to cast a variable into a particular type

Summary

In this chapter, we examined some of the data types available in the R environment. These include discrete data types such as integers and factors. It also includes continuous data types such as real and complex data types. We also examined ways to test a variable to determine what type it is.

In the next chapter, we look at the data structures that can be used to keep track of data. This includes vectors and data types such as lists and data frames that can be constructed from vectors.

2
Organizing Data

In this chapter, we will explore the primary data structures that are used to organize data. Some of the details about accessing information within data structures will be discussed, and some of the ways to apply different operations to parts of the data within a data structure will be discussed too. There are roughly three parts to this chapter:

- **Basic data structures**: This section gives you information on using vectors, lists, data frames, tables, matrices, and time series
- **Accessing and managing memory**: This section gives you an overview of the basic ways to gain access and censor specific elements
- **Operations on data structures**: This section gives you an overview of the operations and methods used to apply operations within the different kinds of data structures

Basic data structures

The basic data structures used to organize data within the R environment include vectors, lists, data frames, tables, and matrices. Here, we provide details for each of these data structures and demonstrate how to create them. This chapter does not include information about how to read data from a file, and the focus is on the data structures themselves. More information about reading from a file can be found in *Chapter 3, Saving Data and Printing Results*.

Vectors

The default data structure in R is the vector. For example, if you define a variable as a single number, R will treat it as a vector of length one:

```
> a <- 5
> a[1]
[1] 5
```

Vectors represent a convenient and straightforward way to store a long list of numbers. Please see *Chapter 1, Data Types*, to see more examples of creating vectors. One useful and common way to define a vector is to use the c command. The c command concatenates a set of arguments to form a single vector:

```
> v <- c(1,3,5,7,-10)
> v
[1]    1    3    5    7 -10
> v[4]
[1] 7
> v[2] <- v[1]-v[5]
> v
[1]    1   11    5    7 -10
```

Two other methods to generate vectors make use of the : notation and the seq command. The : notation is used to create a list of sequentially numbered values for given start and end values. The seq command does the same thing, but it provides more options to determine the increment between values in the vector:

```
> 1:5
[1] 1 2 3 4 5
> 10:14
[1] 10 11 12 13 14
> a <- 3:7
> a
[1] 3 4 5 6 7
> b <- seq(3,5)
> b
[1] 3 4 5
> b <- seq(3,10,by=3)
> b
[1] 3 6 9
```

Lists

Another important type is the list. Lists are flexible and are an unstructured way of organizing information. A list can be thought of as a collection of named objects. A list is created using the list command, and a variable can be tested or coerced using the is.list and as.list commands. A component within a list is accessed using the $ character to denote which object within the list to use. As an example, suppose that we want to create a list to keep track of the parameters for an experiment. The first component, called means, will be a vector of the assumed means. The second component will be the confidence level, and the third component will be the value of a parameter for the experiment called maxRealEigen:

```
> assumedMeans <- c(1.0,1.5,2.1)
> alpha <- 0.05
> eigenValue <- 3+2i
> l <- list(means=assumedMeans,alpha=alpha,maxRealEigen=eigenValue)
> l
$means
[1] 1.0 1.5 2.1
$alpha
[1] 0.05
$maxRealEigen
[1] 3+2i

> l$means
[1] 1.0 1.5 2.1
> l$means[2]
[1] 1.5
```

The names and attributes commands can be used to determine the components within a list. The attributes command is a more generic command that can be used to list the components of classes and a wider range of objects. Note that the names command can also be used to rename the components of a list. In the following example, we use the previous example but change the names of the elements:

```
> l <- list(means=c(1.0,1.5,2.1),alpha=0.05,maxRealEigen=3+2i)
> names(l)
[1] "means"          "alpha"          "maxRealEigen"
> names(l) <- c("assumedMeans","confidenceLevels","maximumRealValue")
> l
$assumedMeans
[1] 1.0 1.5 2.1
$confidenceLevels
[1] 0.05
$maximumRealValue
[1] 3+2i
```

Data frames

A data frame is similar to a list, and many of the operations are similar. The primary difference is that all of the components of a data frame must have the same number of elements. This is one of the most common ways to store information, and many of the functions available to read data from a file return a data frame by default. For example, suppose we ask five people two questions. The first question is, "Do you have a pet cat?" The second question is, "How many rooms in your house need new carpet?":

```
> d <- data.frame(Q1=as.factor(c("y","n","y","y","n")),
+                  Q2=c(2,0,1,2,0))
> d
  Q1 Q2
1  y  2
2  n  0
3  y  1
4  y  2
5  n  0
> d$Q1
[1] y n y y n
Levels: n y
> summary(d)
 Q1            Q2
 n:2    Min.    :0
 y:3    1st Qu.:0
        Median :1
        Mean    :1
        3rd Qu.:2
        Max.    :2
```

The `names` and `attributes` commands have the same behaviors with data frames as lists. In the preceding example, we take the data frame defined in the previous example and rename the fields to something more descriptive:

```
> d <- data.frame(Q1=as.factor(c("y","n","y","y","n")),
+                  Q2=c(2,0,1,2,0))
> names(d) <- c("HaveCat","NumberRooms")
> d
  HaveCat NumberRooms
1    y          2
2    n          0
3    y          1
4    y          2
5    n          0
```

Tables

Tables can be easily constructed and R will automatically generate frequency tables from categorical data. The `table` command has a number of options, but we focus on basic examples here. More details can be found using the `help(table)` command. In the next example, we take the data from the preceding cat questions and create a table from the answers from the first question:

```
> d <- data.frame(Q1=as.factor(c("y","n","y","y","n")),
+                 Q2=c(2,0,1,2,0))
> q1Results <- table(d$Q1)
> q1Results

n y
2 3
> summary(q1Results)
Number of cases in table: 5
Number of factors: 1
```

If you wish to create a two way table, then simply provide two vectors to the table command to get the cross tabulation. Again, we look at the data from the cat questions. Note that we have to convert the second question to a factor:

```
> d <- data.frame(Q1=as.factor(c("y","n","y","y","n")),
+                 Q2=c(2,0,1,2,0))
> results <- table(d$Q1,as.factor(d$Q2))
> results

    0 1 2
  n 2 0 0
  y 0 1 2
> summary(results)
Number of cases in table: 5
Number of factors: 2
Test for independence of all factors:
        Chisq = 5, df = 2, p-value = 0.08208
        Chi-squared approximation may be incorrect
```

The rows and columns of the table have names associated with them, and the `rownames` and `colnames` commands can be used to assign the names. These commands are similar to the `names` command. In the preceding example, the names in the table are not descriptive. In the following example, we build the table and rename the rows and columns:

```
> d <- data.frame(Q1=as.factor(c("y","n","y","y","n")),
+                 Q2=c(2,0,1,2,0))
> results <- table(d$Q1,as.factor(d$Q2))
```

```
> rownames(results) <- c("No Cat","Has Cat")
> colnames(results) <- c("No room","One room","Two rooms")
> results
        No room One room Two rooms
No Cat      2        0        0
Has Cat     0        1        2
```

One last note; the argument to the table command requires ordinal data. If you have numeric data, it can be quickly transformed to encode which interval contains each number. The cut command takes the numeric data and a vector of break points that indicate the cutoff points between each interval, as follows:

```
> a <- c(-0.8,-0.7,0.9,-1.4,-0.3,1.2)
> b <- cut(a,breaks=c(-1.5,-1,-0.5,0,0.5,1.0,1.5))
> b
[1] (-1,-0.5] (-1,-0.5] (0.5,1]   (-1.5,-1] (-0.5,0]  (1,1.5]
Levels: (-1.5,-1] (-1,-0.5] (-0.5,0] (0,0.5] (0.5,1] (1,1.5]
> summary(b)
(-1.5,-1] (-1,-0.5]  (-0.5,0]   (0,0.5]   (0.5,1]   (1,1.5]
        1         2         1         0         1         1
> table(b)
b
(-1.5,-1] (-1,-0.5]  (-0.5,0]   (0,0.5]   (0.5,1]   (1,1.5]
        1         2         1         0         1         1
```

Matrices and arrays

Tables are a special case of an array. An array or a matrix can be constructed directly using either the array or matrix commands. The array command takes a vector and dimensions, and it constructs an array using column major order. If you wish to provide the data in row major order, then the command to transpose the result is t:

```
> a <- c(1,2,3,4,5,6)
> A <- array(a,c(2,3))
> A
     [,1] [,2] [,3]
[1,]    1    3    5
[2,]    2    4    6
> t(A)
     [,1] [,2]
[1,]    1    2
[2,]    3    4
[3,]    5    6
```

You are not limited to two-dimensional arrays. The `dim` option can include any number of dimensions. In the following example, a three-dimensional array is created by using three numbers for the number of dimensions:

```
> A <- array(1:24,c(2,3,4),dimnames=c("row","col","dep"))
> A
, , 1

     [,1] [,2] [,3]
[1,]    1    3    5
[2,]    2    4    6

, , 2

     [,1] [,2] [,3]
[1,]    7    9   11
[2,]    8   10   12

, , 3

     [,1] [,2] [,3]
[1,]   13   15   17
[2,]   14   16   18

, , 4

     [,1] [,2] [,3]
[1,]   19   21   23
[2,]   20   22   24
> A[2,3,4]
[1] 24
```

A matrix is a two-dimensional array and is a special case that can be created using the `matrix` command. Rather than using the dimensions, the `matrix` command requires that you specify the number of rows or columns. The command has an additional option to specify whether or not the data is in row major or column major order:

```
> B <- matrix(1:12,nrow=3)
> B
     [,1] [,2] [,3] [,4]
[1,]    1    4    7   10
[2,]    2    5    8   11
[3,]    3    6    9   12
```

```
> B <- matrix(1:12,nrow=3,byrow=TRUE)
> B
     [,1] [,2] [,3] [,4]
[1,]    1    2    3    4
[2,]    5    6    7    8
[3,]    9   10   11   12
```

Both matrices and arrays can be manipulated to determine or change their dimensions. The dim command can be used to get or set this information:

```
> C <- matrix(1:12,ncol=3)
> C
     [,1] [,2] [,3]
[1,]    1    5    9
[2,]    2    6   10
[3,]    3    7   11
[4,]    4    8   12
> dim(C)
[1] 4 3
> dim(C) <- c(3,4)
> C
     [,1] [,2] [,3] [,4]
[1,]    1    4    7   10
[2,]    2    5    8   11
[3,]    3    6    9   12
```

Censoring data

Using a logical vector as an index is useful for limiting data that is examined. For example, to limit a vector to examine only the positive values in the data set, a logical comparison can be used for the index into the vector:

```
> u <- 1:6
> v <- c(-1,1,-2,2,-3,3)
> u
[1] 1 2 3 4 5 6
> v
[1] -1  1 -2  2 -3  3
> u[v > 0]
[1] 2 4 6
> u[v < 0] = -2*u[v < 0]
> u
[1]  -2   2  -6   4 -10   6
```

Another useful aspect of a logical index into a vector is the use of the NA data type. The is.na function and a logical NOT operator (!) can be a useful tool when a vector contains data that is not defined:

```
> v <- c(1,2,3,NA,4,NA)
> v
[1]  1  2  3 NA  4 NA
> v[is.na(v)]
[1] NA NA
> v[!is.na(v)]
[1] 1 2 3 4
```

Note that many functions have optional arguments to specify how R should react to data that contains a value with the NA type. Unfortunately, the way this is done is not consistent, and you should use the help command with respect to any particular function:

```
> v <- c(1,2,3,NA,4,NA)
> v
[1]  1  2  3 NA  4 NA
> mean(v)
[1] NA
> mean(v,na.rm=TRUE)
[1] 2.5
```

In this last example, the na.rm option in the mean function is set to TRUE to specify that R should ignore the entries in the vector that are NA.

Appending rows and columns

The cbind and rbind commands can be used to append data to existing objects. These commands can be used on vectors, matrices, arrays, and they are extended to also act on data frames. The following examples use data frames, as that is a common operation. You should be careful and try the commands on arrays to make sure that the operation behaves in the way you expect.

The cbind command is used to combine the columns of the data given as arguments:

```
> d <- data.frame(one=c(1,2,3),two=as.factor(c("one","two","three")))
> e <- c("ein","zwei","drei")
> newDataFrame <- cbind(d,third=e)
> newDataFrame
  one   two third
1   1   one   ein
```

```
2   2   two   zwei
3   3 three   drei
> newDataFrame$third
[1] ein   zwei drei
Levels: drei ein zwei
```

If the arguments to the cbind command are two data frames (or two arrays), then the command combines all of the columns from all of the data frames (arrays):

```
> d <- data.frame(one=c(1,2,3),two=as.factor(c("one","two","three")))
> e <- data.frame(three=c(4,5,6),four=as.factor(c("vier","funf","sec
hs")))
> newDataFrame <- cbind(d,e)
> newDataFrame
  one   two three   four
1   1   one     4   vier
2   2   two     5   funf
3   3 three     6 sechs
```

The rbind command concatenates the rows of the objects passed to it. The command uses the names of the columns to determine how to append the data. The number and names of the columns must be identical:

```
> d <- data.frame(one=c(1,2,3),two=as.factor(c("one","two","three")))
> e <- data.frame(one=c(4,5,6),two=as.factor(c("vier","funf","sec
hs")))
> newDataFrame <- rbind(d,e)
> newDataFrame
  one   two
1   1   one
2   2   two
3   3 three
4   4   vier
5   5   funf
6   6 sechs
```

Operations on data structures

The R environment has a rich set of options available for performing operations on data within the various data structures. These operations can be performed in a variety of ways and can be restricted according to various criteria. The focus of this section is the purpose and formats of the various apply commands.

The `apply` commands are used to instruct R to use a given command on specific parts of a list, vector, or array. Each data type has different versions of the `apply` commands that are available. Before discussing the different commands, it is important to define the notion of the margins of a table or array. The margins are defined along any dimension, and the dimension used must be specified. The `margin` command can be used to determine the sum of the row, columns, or the entire column of an array or table:

```
> A <- matrix(1:12,nrow=3,byrow=TRUE)
> A
     [,1] [,2] [,3] [,4]
[1,]    1    2    3    4
[2,]    5    6    7    8
[3,]    9   10   11   12
> margin.table(A)
[1] 78
> margin.table(A,1)
[1] 10 26 42
> margin.table(A,2)
[1] 15 18 21 24
```

The last two commands specify the optional margin argument. The `margin.table(A,1)` command specifies that the sums are in the first dimension, that is, the rows. The `margin.table(A,2)` command specifies that the sums are in the second dimension, that is, the columns. The idea of specifying which dimension to use in a command can be important when using the `apply` commands.

The apply commands

The various `apply` commands are used to operate on the different data structures. Each one—`apply`, `lapply`, `sapply`, `tapply`, and `mapply`—will be briefly discussed in order in the following sections.

apply

The `apply` command is used to apply a given function across a given margin of an array or table. For example, to take the sum of a row or column from a two way table, use the `apply` command with arguments for the table, the `sum` command, and which dimension to use:

```
> A <- matrix(1:12,nrow=3,byrow=TRUE)
> A
     [,1] [,2] [,3] [,4]
[1,]    1    2    3    4
```

```
[2,]     5     6     7     8
[3,]     9    10    11    12
> apply(A,1,sum)
[1] 10 26 42
> apply(A,2,sum)
[1] 15 18 21 24
```

You should be able to verify these results using the `rowSums` and `colSums` commands as well as the `margin.table` command discussed previously.

lapply and sapply

The `lapply` command is used to apply a function to each element in a list. The result is a list, where each component of the returned object is the function applied to the object in the original list with the same name:

```
> theList <- list(one=c(1,2,3),two=c(TRUE,FALSE,TRUE,TRUE))
> sumResult <- lapply(theList,sum)
> sumResult
$one
[1] 6

$two
[1] 3

> typeof(sumResult)
[1] "list"
> sumResult$one
[1] 6
```

The `sapply` command is similar to the `lapply` command, and it performs the same operation. The difference is that the result is coerced to be a vector if possible:

```
> theList <- list(one=c(1,2,3),two=c(TRUE,FALSE,TRUE,TRUE))
> meanResult <- sapply(theList,mean)
> meanResult
 one  two
2.00 0.75
> typeof(meanResult)
[1] "double"
```

tapply

The `tapply` command is used to apply a function to different parts of data within an array. The function takes at least three arguments. The first is the data to apply an operation, the second is the set of factors that defines how the data is organized with respect to the different levels, and the third is the operation to perform. In the following example, a vector is defined that has the diameter of trees. A second vector is defined, which specifies what kind of tree was measured for each observation. The goal is to find the standard deviation for each type of tree:

```
> diameters <- c(28.8, 27.3, 45.8, 34.8, 25.3)
> tree <- as.factor(c("pine","pine","oak","pine","oak"))
> tapply(diameters,tree,sd)
      oak        pine
14.495689   3.968627
```

mapply

The last command to examine is the `mapply` command. The `mapply` command takes a function to apply and a list of arrays. The function takes the first elements of each array and applies the function to that list. It then takes the second elements of each array and applies the function. This is repeated until it goes through every element. Note that if one of the arrays has fewer elements than the others, the `mapply` command will reset and start at the beginning of that array to fill in the missing values:

```
> a <- c(1,2,3)
> b <- c(1,2,3)
> mapply(sum,a,b)
[1] 2 4 6
>
```

Summary

In this chapter, we examined the basic data structures available to help organize data. These data structures include vectors, lists, data frames, tables, and arrays. We examined some of the ways to manage the data structures using the `rbind` and `cbind` commands. Finally, we examined some of the methods available to perform calculations on the data within the data structure and examined the various functions available to apply commands to parts of the data within the data structure.

In the next chapter, we will build on these ideas and examine how to get information from a data file and into the various data structures. We will also examine the methods available to produce formatted output to display the results of calculations on data.

3
Saving Data and Printing Results

This chapter provides you with a broad overview of the ways to get information into as well as out of the R environment. There are various packages that are available and related to this important function, but we will focus on a subset of the basic, built-in functions. The chapter is divided into the following five sections:

- **File and directory information**: This section gives you a brief overview of how files and directories are organized in the R environment

- **Input**: This section gives you an overview of the methods that can be used to bring data into the R environment

- **Output**: This section gives you an overview of the methods available to get data out of the R environment

- **Primitive input/output**: This section gives you an overview of the methods you can use to write data in binary or character forms in predefined formats

- **Network options**: This section gives you a brief overview of the methods associated with creating and manipulating sockets

File and directory information

Before discussing how to save or read data, we first need to examine R's facilities for getting information about files and directories. We will first discuss the commands used to work with directories and files, and then discuss the commands used to manipulate the current working directory. The basic commands to list directory and file information are the `dir`, `list.dirs`, and `list.files` commands. The basic commands to list and change the current working directory are `getwd` and `setwd`.

The `dir`, `list.dirs`, and `list.files` commands are used to get information about directories and files within directories. By default, the commands will get information about the directories in the current working directory:

```
> dir()
[1] "R"     "bin" "csv"
> d <- dir()
> d[1]
[1] "R"
```

The preceding commands also accept a wide variety of options. Use of the `help` command is recommended to see more details:

```
> list.files('./csv')
[1] "network.csv" "trees.csv"
> f <- list.files('./csv')
> f[2]
[1] "trees.csv"
```

These commands have an optional parameter for specifying a pattern, and the pattern is a regular expression. The topic of regular expressions is beyond the scope of this discussion, but it offers a very powerful option for specifying a filter to determine the names of files. For example, all of the files that begin with the letter n can be easily determined:

```
> f <- list.files('./csv',pattern='^n')
> f
[1] "network.csv"
```

Another important topic is the idea of the current working directory. When the R environment seeks a file or directory whose name is given in a relative form, it starts from the current working directory. There are several other ways to specify the current directory, and it is part of the majority of graphical interfaces. Unfortunately, it varies across the different interfaces.

The commands to manipulate the current working directory via the command line are the `getwd` and `setwd` commands. The names of directories (folders) are separated using forward slashes:

```
> getwd()
[1] "/tmp/examples"
> d <- getwd()
> d
[1] "/tmp/examples"
```

Entering data

Having discussed the ideas associated with directories and files, we can now discuss how to read data. Here, we will provide an overview of the different ways to get information from a file. We will begin with a short overview about entering data from the command line followed by examples for reading a text file in the form of a table, from a `csv` file, and fixed width files. Finally, we will discuss more primitive methods to read from a binary file.

It is important to note that we rely on the topics discussed in *Chapter 1, Data Types* and *Chapter 2, Organizing Data*. I assume that you are familiar with the various data types given in *Chapter 1, Data Types*, as well as the data structures discussed in *Chapter 2, Organizing Data*. In this chapter, we will explore a small number of ways to read data into R. There are a large number of libraries available to read data in a wide variety of formats such as JSON, XML, SAS, Excel, and other file formats. There are also more options available in the base R distribution. To see more options, type `read` and press the *TAB* key (no space after the letters `read`) to see a partial list of other options.

Entering data from the command line

We will examine two ways to read data including reading keyboard input from the command line and reading data from a file. We first examine some techniques used to obtain information through the command line. More details can be found in *Chapter 2, Organizing Data*, and we will explore additional ways to enter data including the use of the `scan` and `data.entry` commands.

In addition to concatenating information with the `c` command, there are additional commands to make it easier to define data. The first command we will examine is the `scan` command. If you simply assign a variable using the `scan` command with no arguments, then you are prompted and required to enter the numbers from the command line. If you enter a blank line (just hit the *Enter* key), then the previous values are returned as a vector:

```
> x <- scan()
1: 28.8
2: 27.3
3: 45.8
4: 34.8
5: 23.5
6:
Read 5 items
> x
[1] 28.8 27.3 45.8 34.8 23.5
```

In this example, the `scan` command is used to prompt us to enter a set of numbers. After a blank entry is given, the command returns a vector with the previous values.

If you provide a filename, then the `scan` command will read the values from the file as if you had typed them on the command line. Suppose that we have a file called `diameters.csv` with the following contents:

```
28.8
27.3
45.8
34.8
25.3
```

You can read the contents using the `scan` command as follows:

```
> x <- scan("diameters.csv")
Read 5 items
> x
[1] 28.8 27.3 45.8 34.8 25.3
```

You can read more complex data from a file using the `scan` command, but you must specify the structure of the file. This means that you have to specify the data types. Here, assume that we have a data file called `trees.csv`:

```
pine,28.8
pine,27.3
oak,45.8
pine,34.8
oak,25.3
```

The first column is the character data, and the second column is the numeric data. The information on each line is separated by a comma. The `scan` command assumes that the information is separated using white space (spaces and tabs), so in this case, we have to specify that a comma is used as the separator within the file. In the following example, the file is read, and the format is given using the `what` argument:

```
> x <- scan("trees.csv",what=list("character","double"),sep=",")
Read 5 records
> x
[[1]]
[1] "pine" "pine" "oak"  "pine" "oak"

[[2]]
[1] "28.8" "27.3" "45.8" "34.8" "25.3"
```

Another method for entering data is to use the `data.entry` command. The command will open up a graphical interface if it is available on your system. The details can vary depending on your operating system and the graphical interface that you are using.

Reading tables from files

One common method used to read data from a file is to read it as a table. This assumes that the file is nicely formatted and arranged in convenient rows and columns. A command to read data in this form is the `read.table` command. There are a large number of options for this command, and it is highly recommended that you use the `help` command, `help(read.table)`, to see more complete details about this command.

The first example demonstrates how to read a simple file. It is assumed that you have a file called `trialTable.dat` in the following format:

```
1 2 3
3 5 6
```

The file has no header, and the values are separated by spaces (white space). In this simple format, the file can be read with the default options:

```
> trial <- read.table("trialTable.dat")
> trial
  V1 V2 V3
1  1  2  3
2  3  5  6
> typeof(trial)
[1] "list"
> names(trial)
[1] "V1" "V2" "V3"
```

The result is a list of values. No names were specified for the names of the columns, and the default values for the column names have been used.

CSV files

The `read.table` command offers a general way to read the data from a file with a known structure. One common file structure is a file where the values are separated by commas, or a `csv` file. The command to read a `csv` file is the `read.csv` command. There is an alternate version of the command, `read.csv2`, which has a different set of defaults. The difference is that the defaults for `read.csv2` are defined to allow a simple way of reading a file in which the delimiter between the decimal values is a comma and the values are separated by semicolons, which are more commonly used in some European countries.

The `read.csv` command is similar to the `read.table` command. The primary difference is that the result is returned as a data frame, and a greater range of data types for the columns are recognized.

In the preceding examples, the `trialTable.csv` file is read into the workspace. The same file can be read using the `read.csv` command. The `trialTable.csv` file does not have a header, and the numbers are separated using spaces:

```
> trial <- read.csv("trialTable.csv",header=FALSE,sep=' ')
> trial
  V1 V2 V3
1  1  2  3
2  3  5  6
> typeof(trial)
[1] "list"
```

In the next example, we have a data file in which each line has the same number of columns, and the data fields are separated by commas. The file was downloaded from http://www.bea.gov/. The first six lines of the file are used to identify information about the data in a human-readable form, but that information should be ignored by the `read.csv` function. The other thing to note is that the seventh line is a header; it has information that defines the label used to refer to the columns. The last thing to note is that the numbers are separated by commas. All of these details must be specified if we want to read the file using the `read.csv` command. This second file, `inventories.csv`, can be read using the `read.csv` command, as follows:

```
inventories <- read.csv("inventories.csv", +
skip=6,header=TRUE,sep=",")
> typeof(inventories)
[1] "list"
> names(inventories)
 [1] "Line"    "X"       "X1994.1" "X1994.2" "X1994.3" "X1994.4"
"X1995.1"
 [8] "X1995.2" "X1995.3" "X1995.4" "X1996.1" "X1996.2" "X1996.3"
"X1996.4"
```

Fixed-width files

Another common file format is a fixed width file. In a fixed width file, every line has the same format and the information within a given line is strictly organized by columns. A file in this format can be read using the `read.fwf` command. To use the `read.fwf` command, you must specify the name of the file and the width of each column. You can instruct R to ignore a column by providing a negative value for the width of the column.

In this example, we assume that a file with the name `trialFWF.dat` is in the current working directory. The contents of the file are as follows:

```
12312345121234
B      100ZZ  18
C      200YY  20
D      300XX  22
```

The first three columns are assumed to contain letters, the next five columns contain numbers, the next two columns have letters, and the last four columns are numbers. In the example file, the top row should be ignored as it is used to demonstrate how the file is organized. The `skip` option is used to indicate how many lines to ignore at the top of the file:

```
> trial <- read.fwf('trialFWF.dat',c(3,5,2,4),skip=1)
> trial
   V1   V2 V3 V4
1 B    100 ZZ 18
2 C    200 YY 20
3 D    300 XX 22
> trial$V1
[1] B   C   D
Levels: B   C   D
```

Note that when a width is given as a negative number, that column is ignored:

```
> trial <- read.fwf('trialFWF.dat',c(3,-5,2,4),skip=1)
> trial
   V1 V2 V3
1 B    ZZ 18
2 C    YY 20
3 D    XX 22
```

Printing results and saving data

We will explore the options available to take information stored within the R environment and express that information in either human- or machine-readable forms. We will start with a brief discussion on saving the workspace in an R environment. Next, we will discuss various commands that can be used to print information to either the screen or a file. Finally, we will discuss the primitive commands that can be used for basic file operations.

Saving a workspace

There are two commands used to save the information in the current workspace. The first is the `save` command, which allows you to save particular variables. The second is the `save.image` command, which allows you to save all the variables within the workspace.

The `save` command requires a list of variables to save, and the name of a file to save the variables. There are a wide variety of options, but in the most basic form you simply save specific variables from the current workspace. Here, we use the `ls` command to first list the variables in the current workspace and then use the `save` command to save two variables, `inventories` and `trees`:

```
> dir()
[1] "diameters.csv"   "inventories.csv" "network.csv"  "trees.csv"
[5] "trialFWF.dat"    "trialTable.csv"
> ls()
[1] "a"        "d"        "f"           "inventories" "trees"
[6] "trial"    "x"        "y"
> save(inventories,trees,file="theInventories.RData")
> dir()
[1] "diameters.csv"          "inventories.csv"      "network.csv"
[4] "theInventories.RData"   "trees.csv"            "trialFWF.dat"
[7] "trialTable.csv"
```

The `save.image` command requires only one argument; the name of the file used to save the information:

```
> dir()
[1] "diameters.csv"          "inventories.csv"      "network.csv"
[4] "theInventories.RData"   "trees.csv"            "trialFWF.dat"
[7] "trialTable.csv"
> save.image("wholeShebang.RData")
> dir()
```

```
[1]  "diameters.csv"          "inventories.csv"          "network.csv"
[4]  "theInventories.RData"   "trees.csv"                "trialFWF.dat"
[7]  "trialTable.csv"         "wholeShebang.RData"
```

If you start a new R session, the information that has been saved using a `save` or `save.image` command can be read using the `load` command:

```
> ls()
character(0)
> dir()
[1]  "diameters.csv"          "inventories.csv"          "network.csv"
[4]  "theInventories.RData"   "trees.csv"                "trialFWF.dat"
[7]  "trialTable.csv"         "wholeShebang.RData"
> load("theInventories.RData")
> ls()
[1]  "inventories"  "trees"
```

The cat command

The `cat` command can be used to take a list of variables, convert them to a text form, and concatenate the results. If no file or connector is specified, the result is printed to the screen; otherwise, the connector is used to determine how the result is handled. Note that there is an additional set of commands, the various write commands, but those commands are convenient routines that allow a shorthand notation to access the `cat` commands. These commands are primarily used in scripts:

```
> one <- "A"
> two <- "B"
> cat(one,two,"\n")
A B
```

The `cat` command allows you to specify a number of options. For example, you can specify the separator between variables, labels to be used, or whether or not to append to a given file:

```
> cat(one,two,"\n",sep=" - ")
A - B -
```

The print, format, and paste commands

We examine three ways to display information using the `print`, `format`, and `paste` commands. These can be used by programs to display the formatted output. The three commands provide numerous options to ensure that the information appears in human-readable forms.

The `print` command is used to display the contents of a single variable, as follows:

```
> one <- "A"
> print(one)
[1] "A"
```

The `paste` command takes a list of variables, converts them to characters, and concatenates the result. This is a useful command to dynamically create annotations for plots and figures, as follows:

```
> one <- "A"
> two <- "B"
> numbers <- paste(one,two)
> numbers
[1] "A B"
> numbers <- paste(one,two,sep="/")
> numbers
[1] "A/B"
```

In this example, the `numbers` variable is a string, and it is the result of converting the arguments to a string and concatenating the results. In the second part of the example, the separator was changed from the default, a space, to a forward slash.

The `format` command converts an R object to a string, and it allows a large number of options to specify the appearance of the object:

```
> three <- exp(1)
> nice <- format(three,digits=2)
> nice
[1] "2.7"
> nice <- format(three,digits=12)
> nice
[1] "2.71828182846"
> nice <- format(three,digits=3,width=5,justify="right")
> nice
[1] " 2.72"
> nice <- format(three,digits=3,width=8,justify="right",decimal.
mark="#")
> nice
[1] "    2#72"
```

In this example, the `format` command is used in various ways to convert a numeric variable to a string. The various options to change the number of digits and the total number of characters has been changed to refine the results.

Primitive input/output

There are a number of primitive commands that offer fine grain control for reading and writing information to and from a file. We do not provide extensive examples here because these commands are more useful when combined with the programming commands that are explored in later chapters.

Before discussing these commands, it is important to discuss the idea of a connector. A connector is a generic way to treat a data source. This can be a file, an HTTP connection, a database connection, or another network connection. In this section, we only explore one type of connector, that is, the basic text file connector. More information can be found using the `help` command, `help(file)`. The `file` command is used to create a connector to a file. The arguments to the `file` command are similar to the `fopen` command found in the C language.

The most basic use of the `file` command requires that you provide a name of a file and the mode that will be used in manipulating the file. The mode can tell R whether the file will be used to read or write as well as whether or not it is a binary file. In this first example, we will open a file and write a double precision number and then a character string. In the next example that follows, we will open the file and read the information back into the workspace. To write the information, we will first use the `file` command to open a file, call `twoBinaryValues.dat`, and use the binary mode. We will then use the `writeBin` command to write the two values. We assume here that a double precision number requires four bytes:

```
> fileConnector = file("twoBinaryValues.dat",open="wb")
> theNumber = as.double(2.72)
> writeBin(theNumber,fileConnector,size=4)
> note <- "hello there!"
> nchar(note)
[1] 12
> writeBin(note,fileConnector,size=nchar(note))
> close(fileConnector)
```

In this example, a file connector is created to write information in a binary format. Two variables are then written to the file, and the file is closed. The same information is read in the next example. The `readBin` command is used to read the information from the file:

```
> fileConnector = file("twoBinaryValues.dat",open="rb")
> value <- readBin(fileConnector,double(),1,size=4)
> value
[1] 2.72
> note <- readBin(fileConnector,character(),12,size=1)
```

```
> note
[1] "hello there!"
> close(fileConnector)
```

There are a number of commands that can be used to read and write character data. The writeChar and readChar commands are used to write and read character data in a similar way as the writeBin and readBin commands. The writeLines and readLines commands can be used to write whole lines as characters at one time.

Network options

Another way to read information is through a network connection using sockets. The methods available to manipulate sockets will be briefly explored in this section. We first explore the high level socket commands that make use of the socketConnection command to create a connector. Next, some of the more basic options are briefly stated. This is an advanced topic beyond the scope of this book, but it is provided here as a matter of completeness.

Opening a socket

The socketConnection command will create a network connection to a given host using a port number. The command returns a connector that can be treated the same as a file connector. In the following example, a connection is opened to the waterdata.usgs.gov website using the standard HTTP port, 80. It then sends the HTTP header necessary to request the data for the daily flow rates for the South Colton station on the Raquette River in northern New York:

```
> usgs <- socketConnection(host = "waterdata.usgs.gov",80)
> writeLines("GET /ny/nwis/dv?cb_00060=on&format=rdb&site_
no=04267500&referred_module=sw&period=&begin_date=2013-05-08&end_
date=2014-05-08 HTTP/1.1",con=usgs)
> writeLines("Host: waterdata.usgs.gov",con=usgs)
> writeLines("\n\n",con=usgs)
> lines = readLines(usgs)
> lines
   [1] "HTTP/1.1 200 OK"
   [2] "Date: Fri, 09 May 2014 16:28:26 GMT"
   [3] "Server: Apache"
   [4] "AMF-Ver: 4.02"
   [5] "Connection: close"
   [6] "Transfer-Encoding: chunked"
   [7] "Content-Type: text/plain"
   [8] ""
```

```
    [9]  "3bc"
    [10] "# --------------------------------- WARNING ------------------
    ---------------------"
    [11] "# The data you have obtained from this automated U.S.
    Geological Survey database"
    [12] "# have not received Director's approval and as such are
    provisional and subject to"
    [13] "# revision.  The data are released on the condition that
    neither the USGS nor the"
    [14] "# United States Government may be held liable for any damages
    resulting from its use."
    [15] "# Additional info: http://waterdata.usgs.gov/ny/nwis/?provisio
    nal"
    [16] "#"
    [17] "# File-format description:  http://waterdata.usgs.gov/
    nwis/?tab_delimited_format_info"
    [18] "# Automated-retrieval info: http://help.waterdata.usgs.gov/faq/
    automated-retrievals"
    [19] "#"
    [20] "# Contact:   gs-w_support_nwisweb@usgs.gov"
    [21] "# retrieved: 2014-05-09 12:28:35 EDT        (vaww01)"
    [22] "#"
    [23] "# Data for the following 1 site(s) are contained in this file"
    [24] "#    USGS 04267500 RAQUETTE RIVER AT SOUTH COLTON NY"

...[Deleted Lines]...

    [425] "USGS\t04267500\t2014-05-07\t5810\tP"
    [426] "USGS\t04267500\t2014-05-08\t5640\tP"
    [427] ""
    [428] "0"
    [429] ""
> close(usgs)
```

In this example, a socket connection is created. It is used to make a connection to a URL with a given port. The socket connector is then used to send an HTTP header to request a particular page from the given host. The resulting page is read using the readLines command. The readLines command is used to read every line as a string, and the information in the vector will have to be parsed to transform it into a useable form.

Basic socket operations

Aside from the higher level option given in the previous section, there are also more primitive commands for creating and using a socket. The commands examined are the `make.socket`, `read.socket`, `write.socket`, and the `close.socket` commands. Sockets are scarce resources, and checks need to be put in place to ensure that they are released when something goes wrong. For that reason, a socket is usually created within a function with extra checks. The example here is basic, and it is provided simply to demonstrate the commands. You should see the help pages for the socket commands for a more comprehensive example.

To replicate the preceding example, the socket is opened, and the HTTP request is submitted:

```
> socketRead <- make.socket("waterdata.usgs.gov",80)
> write.socket(socketRead,"GET /ny/nwis/
dv?cb_00060=on&format=rdb&site_no=04267500&referred_
module=sw&period=&begin_date=2013-05-08&end_date=2014-05-08
HTTP/1.1\n");
> write.socket(socketRead,"Host: waterdata.usgs.gov\n\n\n");
> incoming <- read.socket(socketRead);
> close.socket(socketRead)
[1] FALSE
```

The `incoming` variable will now contain the result of the operation.

Summary

In this chapter, we have explored some of the facilities available to read and write information to a file as well as ways to enter data from the command line. We examined the ways to change between directories and get the directory information.

After examining ways to read data, we explored some of the ways that the information can be displayed. We first examined how to print information on the command line, and we then explored how to save data to a local file. We also explored how the current work space could be saved and recalled for use in a later session.

One important topic explored was how to work with files that do not follow a basic format. We examined the commands necessary to read data, in both text and binary forms where the data file follows a predefined structure.

The final topic explored was how to use network connections to read information. This included the use of a socket connector to allow access to relatively well-structured information. We also explored more primitive options that allow us to create sockets and manipulate them in a more basic form.

In the previous chapters, we examined the basic ways to store data. In the chapter that follows, *Chapter 4, Calculating Probabilities and Random Numbers*, we get our first glimpse of the functions available to help us understand how to interpret data. We will explore some of the options available to work with various predefined probability distributions.

4

Calculating Probabilities and Random Numbers

In this chapter, we provide a broad overview of the functions related to probability distributions. This includes functions associated with probability distributions, Random Number Generation, and issues associated with sampling. The chapter is divided into five parts:

- **Distribution functions**: This section gives you a brief overview of the ideas and concepts behind random variables and approximating the height of a probability mass function of a probability density function for a given distribution

- **The cumulative distribution function**: This section gives you an overview of how to approximate the cumulative distribution for a given distribution

- **The inverse cumulative distribution function**: This section gives you an overview of how to approximate the inverse cumulative distribution function for a given distribution

- **Random Number Generation (RNG)**: This section gives you an overview of how R generates pseudorandom numbers with examples of how to generate random numbers for a given distribution

- **Sampling**: This section gives you an overview of sampling data from a given vector

Overview

The base R environment has options for approximating many of the properties associated with probability distributions. This is not a complete discussion, and a more complete list can be found within the R environment using the `help(Distributions)` command. In this chapter, we will discuss how R can be used to approximate distribution functions, how to approximate cumulative distribution functions, how to approximate inverse cumulative distribution functions, **Random Number Generation (RNG)**, and sampling.

The commands used for the first set of topics have a common format, and each command has the form of a prefix and a suffix. The suffix specifies the distribution by name. For example, the `norm` suffix refers to the normal distribution. A list of the distributions available in the base R installation is given in *Table 1*. The prefix is one of the following:

- `d`: This determines the value of the distribution function, for example, `dnorm` is the height of the normal's probability distribution function
- `p`: This determines the cumulative distribution, for example, `pnorm` is the cumulative distribution function for the normal distribution
- `q`: This determines the inverse cumulative distribution, for example, `qnorm` is the inverse cumulative distribution function for the normal distribution
- `r`: This generates random numbers according to the distribution, for example, `rnorm` calculates random numbers that follow a normal distribution

As an example, to determine the probability that a Poisson distribution will return a given value, the command to use is `dpois`, and the command to get the probability that a Poisson distribution is less than or equal to a particular value is `ppois`.

In this chapter, we assume that you are familiar with the idea of a random variable. In short, a random variable is a function, and the function assigns a number for each outcome in the sample space associated with an experiment. A continuous random variable is a function that can include a continuous range of values in the values it can return. A discrete random variable can only return numbers from a discrete set of values. The following table shows the distributions available in R:

Discrete		Continuous	
Name	**Suffix**	**Name**	**Suffix**
Beta	beta	χ^2	chisq
Binomial	binom	Exponential	exp
Cauchy	cauchy	F	f
Geometric	geom	Gamma	gamma
Hypergeometric	hyper	Log Normal	lnorm
Multinomial	mutlinom	Normal	norm
Negative Binomial	nbinom	Student t	t
Poisson	pois	Uniform	unif
		Weibull	weibull

Table 1 – a list of distributions and the suffix used in R to refer to them

Distribution functions

We will first discuss the way to calculate the value of a distribution function in R. We will then discuss discrete distributions and then continuous distributions. The distribution function is used to determine the probabilities that a particular event will occur. In the case of a discrete distribution, the function is called a probability mass function, and for a continuous distribution it is called a probability distribution function. For a discrete distribution, the probabilities are calculated using a sum where *f(i)* is the probability mass function:

$$p\left(a \leq x \leq b\right) = \sum_{i=a}^{b} f\left(i\right),$$

Each distribution has its own parameters associated with it, and judicial use of the help command is highly recommended. For example, to get more information about the Poisson distribution, the `help(dpois)` command can be used. In the case of the Poisson distribution, there are two parameters required for the `dpois` command. The first is x and the second is `lambda`. The function returns the probabilities that a Poisson random variable with the `lambda` parameter returns the values given by x.

For example, to plot the probabilities for a Poisson distribution with parameter 10, the following commands are used to generate the values that can be returned (called x), and a bar plot is used to display them:

```
> x <- 0:20
> probabilities <- dpois(x,10.0)
> barplot(probabilities,names.arg=x,xlab="x",ylab="p", +
  main="Poission Dist, l=10.0")
```

For the continuous distribution, the random variable can take on a range of values, and instead of adding, we find the area under a curve, $f(s)$, called the probability density function:

$$p(b \leq x \leq a) = \int_a^b f(s)\,ds.$$

In the next example, we use the χ^2 distribution. The idea behind the χ^2 distribution is that you sample n independent random variables that follow a standard normal distribution. You then square the values that were sampled and add them up. The result is defined to be an χ^2 distribution. Note that there is one parameter, n, and it is generally specified by giving the *number of degrees of freedom*, which is defined to be n-1. The number of degrees of freedom is often referred to as *df*.

For this example, the command to obtain an approximation for the probability density function is dchisq, and it takes two arguments, x and df. Here, we plot the probability density function for two χ^2 distributions with two different parameters. First a range of values, x, is defined, and then the height of the probability density function for an χ^2 distribution with df=30 is plotted. Next, another χ^2 distribution with df=35 is plotted on the same plot using the points command:

```
> x <- seq(0.0,100.0,by=0.1)
> prob <- dchisq(x,df=30)
> plot(x,prob,main="Chi Squared Dist.",xlab='x',ylab='p',col=2,type=
  "l")
> probTwo <- dchisq(x,df=35)
> points(x,probTwo,col=3,type="l")
```

Cumulative distribution functions

Another important tool used to approximate probabilities is the cumulative distribution function. In many situations, we are required to determine the probability that a random variable will return a value within some given range of values. The cumulative distribution allows us to use a shortcut to calculate the resulting probability. As in the previous section, we look at discrete and continuous distributions separately. We examine the definition and look at examples for both cases.

For a discrete distribution, the cumulative distribution function is defined to be the following equation:

$$F(a) = p(x \leq a) = \sum_{i=-\infty}^{a} f(i).$$

From this definition, the probability that a random variable is between two numbers can be determined by the following equation:

$$p(a \leq x < b) = F(a) - F(b).$$

Please note the details in the inequality. In the case of discrete distributions, it matters if *less than or equal* is used as opposed to *less than*.

For a Poisson distribution, the command to determine the cumulative distribution function is the `ppois` command, and it has the same arguments as the `dpois` command discussed earlier. The following example mirrors the example in the previous section, and the cumulative distribution function is plotted for a Poisson distribution with parameter `10.0`:

```
> x <- 0:20
> cdf <- ppois(x,10.0)
> barplot(cdf,names.arg=x)
```

The cumulative distribution function for a continuous random variable is defined in the same way as that of a discrete random variable. The only difference is that instead of a sum we use an integral, as follows:

$$F(a) - p(x \leq a) \int_{-\infty}^{a} f(s) ds.$$

This definition gives the same result as before, and the probability that a random variable is between two numbers can be determined by using the following equation:

$$p(a \le x < b) = F(a) - F(b).$$

The following example compares the cumulative distribution functions for two χ^2 distributions where the first has 30 degrees of freedom and the second has 35 degrees of freedom:

```
> x <- seq(0.0,100.0,by=0.1)
> cdf <- pchisq(x,df=30)
> plot(x,cdf,main="Chi Squared Dist.",xlab='x',ylab='p',col=2,
+       type="l")
> cdfTwo <- pchisq(x,df=35)
> points(x,cdfTwo,col=3,type="l")
```

Inverse cumulative distribution functions

The cumulative distribution function is often used to calculate probabilities, but in other circumstances the goal is to find a range of values given the probability. In this case, the inverse cumulative distribution function can be used to determine a value of the random variable that corresponds to a given probability. The idea is that given the probability, you want to solve for the value of *a* in the expression:

$$p = p(x \le a) = F(a)$$

For example, suppose that we have a Poisson random variable with parameter `10.0` and wish to find the value of *a* for which the probability of the random variable is less than *a* is 0.5. Using the `qpois` command, we can determine the value:

```
> a <- qpois(0.5,10.0)
> a
[1] 10
```

This result indicates that the probability that a Poisson random variable with parameter 10.0 is less than 10.0 is 0.5, or put another way the median is 10.0. Since this is also the mean of the random variable, we can see that there is no skew associated with the distribution.

We now do the same for the χ^2 distribution with 30 degrees of freedom. The `qchisq` command can be used to determine the median for this distribution:

```
> a <- qchisq(0.5,df=30)
> a
[1] 29.33603
```

In this case, we see that the median is less than the mean, which is 30, so the χ^2 distribution with 30 degrees of freedom is skewed to the left since the median is to the left of the mean.

Generating pseudorandom numbers

A common task in simulations is to generate random numbers that follow a given distribution. We explore this important topic, but it is important to make a few notes about Random Number Generation. First, and foremost, despite the nomenclature, the numbers are not random because they are generated using a deterministic algorithm. Secondly, when debugging and comparing code used to simulate a stochastic process, it is important to be able to generate numbers in a repeatable way to ensure that the results are consistent.

Before discussing generating random numbers, we provide some minimal background information about how R generates random numbers. This is a complex topic, and you can find more details using the `help(RNG)` command. One thing to note is that the `.Random.seed` variable has the value of the current seed, but it is not defined until you do so explicitly or a command is called that requires that a random number be generated. The variable can be set directly, but it is better to change it using the `set.seed` command. Also, the algorithm that is used to generate random numbers can be set or obtained using the `RNGkind` command. Note that the `save` command can be used as a convenient way to save the seed if repeatability of your results is important as you make changes to established code.

Random Number Generation can be a daunting subject, but we primarily focus on how to generate random numbers according to a given distribution. As before, we first examine a discrete distribution; the Poisson distribution with parameter 10.0. We then examine an χ^2 distribution with 30 degrees of freedom. In each case, we generate one hundred random numbers and create a histogram of the results.

First we examine the discrete distribution. The `rpois` command can be used to generate the number. It takes two parameters, the number of points to approximate and the parameter associated with the distribution:

```
> numbers <- rpois(100,10.0)
> hist(numbers,main="100 Samples of a Poisson Dist.",xlab="x")
```

Likewise, a χ^2 distribution can also be sampled, and the results are plotted using a histogram:

```
> numbers <- rchisq(100,df=30)
> hist(numbers,main="100 Samples from a Chi-Squared Dist.",xlab="x")
```

Sampling

The final topic that we will discuss is sampling. This can also be a complicated subject, and it is often used in bootstrapping and a wide variety of other techniques. Because of its prevalence, we provide it as a separate section.

The sole focus of this section is on the `sample` command. It may seem odd to grant such attention to a single command, but sampling is a complex topic with more opinions associated with it than there are statisticians. The `sample` command requires at least one argument, a vector or a number, and it returns a set of values chosen at random. The options for the command allow you to specify how many samples to take, whether or not to use replacement, and a probability distribution if you do not wish to use a uniform mass function.

The `sample` function's behavior depends on whether or not you give it a vector or a number. If you pass a number to it (that is, a vector of length 1), it will sample from the set of whole, positive numbers less than or equal to that number:

```
> sample(3)
[1] 3 2 1
> sample(5)
[1] 2 3 1 4 5
> sample(5.6)
[1] 5 1 4 3 2
```

If you pass it a vector whose length is greater than 1, it will sample from the elements in the vector:

```
> x <- c(1,3,5,7)
> sample(x)
[1] 7 1 5 3
```

If you do not specify the number of samples to take, it will use the number of objects passed to it. The size parameter allows you to specify a different number of samples:

```
> x <- c(1,3,5,7)
> sample(x,size=2)
[1] 1 7
> sample(x,size=3)
[1] 1 3 5
> sample(x,size=8)
Error in sample.int(length(x), size, replace, prob) :
  cannot take a sample larger than the population when 'replace =
FALSE'
```

In the preceding example, the number of samples is larger than the number of elements available. To avoid an error, you have to specify sampling with replacement:

```
> x <- c(1,3,5,7)
> sample(x,size=8,replace=TRUE)
[1] 3 5 5 5 3 7 5 1
```

In the previous examples, the samples were found using the default algorithm. The default is to use a uniform probability mass function meaning every element has the same likelihood of being chosen. You can change this behavior by specifying a vector of probabilities that has the likelihood of choosing each particular element of the vector:

```
> x <- c(1,3,5,7)
> sample(x,size=8,replace=TRUE,p=c(0.05,.10,.15,.70))
[1] 7 3 3 7 7 7 7 5
```

Summary

In this chapter, we examined a broad overview of some of the probability functions in the base R installation. These include functions to approximate the distribution function, the cumulative distribution function, and the inverse cumulative distribution. We also examined how to generate pseudo-random numbers for the various distributions. The final topic explored was the use of the `sample` command, which is used for sampling from a given dataset stored as a vector.

In the next chapter, we step back from the more mathematical ideas explored in this chapter and look at the programming facilities that can be used to manipulate strings. This is an important topic as it is not uncommon for datasets to include string variables, and it is often necessary to extract or add information to the variables within a dataset.

5
Character and String Operations

This chapter will provide you with a broad overview of the operations available for the manipulation of character and string objects. This is a relatively concise chapter, and the focus is on basic operations. There are roughly two parts in this chapter:

- **Basic string operations**: This section gives you a broad overview of the most basic string operations
- **Regular expressions**: This section gives you a brief introduction of three commands that make use of regular expressions

Basic string operations

In some situations, data is kept in the form of characters or strings, whereas in some other situations the strings must be parsed or investigated as part of a statistical analysis. Because of the prevalence of data in the form of strings, the R language has a rich set of options available for manipulating strings. In this chapter, we investigate some of the options available, and our investigation is divided into two parts. They are as follows:

- In the first part, we examine a number of basic string operations whose function is focused on particular operations
- In the second part, we examine the functions that are based on regular expressions that offer a powerful set of wide ranging operations

The use of regular expressions represent a powerful set of tools for string manipulation, but the cost is greater complexity. In this chapter, we only focus on the most basic uses of these functions as their most common uses tend to be parts of more complex code that may use a complicated combination of the commands.

As a way to make the connection between the commands, we assume a common data set throughout this chapter. In particular, we assume that we have a set of URLs:

```
> urls <- c("https://duckduckgo.com?q=Johann+Carl+Friedrich+Gauss",
    "https://search.yahoo.com/search?p=Jean+Baptiste+Joseph+Fourier",
    "http://www.bing.com/search?q=Isaac+Newton",
    "http://www.google.com/search?q=Brahmagupta")
```

We will examine various ways to pull information from each URL. Such a task may be necessary either to pull information from a website or to perform an analysis on the URLs themselves.

Six focused tasks

We first examine six specific tasks. These operations are to determine the length of a string, location of a substring, extract or replace a substring, change the case of a string, split a string into separate parts, and express a combination of objects as a single string. Please note that the examples will make extensive use of the definition of the url vector that is defined in the previous section.

Determining the length of a string

The nchar command is used to determine the length of a string. This option can be used as part of a simple statistic for a set of strings or can be part of a programming tool when it is necessary to iterate over a string. You can specify how the count is calculated with options to count the number of characters, bytes, or width of the resulting string. In most cases, these values will be the same but can differ depending on the Unicode settings for your environment:

```
> nchar(urls)
[1] 52 62 41 42
```

The `nchar` command tries to coerce its argument to a string, which means that it interprets the values of objects whose type is NA as the string NA. Another side effect is that it can return an error when used on factors:

```
>> nchar(c("one",NA,1234))
[1] 3 2 4
> nchar(as.factor(c("a","b","a","a","b","c")))
Error in nchar(as.factor(c("a", "b", "a", "a", "b", "c"))) :
  'nchar()' requires a character vector
```

If you are running R within a Unicode environment such as UTF-8, this command may return an error. If this is the case, try the `allowNA=TRUE` option to see whether the results are appropriate.

One last note; there is an additional command, `nzchar`, which tests to determine whether the character width of the string has zero length. This function returns a logical value, and it is true if the string does not have a zero length. As an example, suppose you have a list of file types with an empty string being an unrecognized file type. You may want to use `nzchar` to create a mask to skip or ignore an empty string:

```
> fileTypes <- c("txt","","html","txt")
> nzchar(fileTypes)
[1]  TRUE FALSE  TRUE  TRUE
> fileTypes[nzchar(fileTypes)]
[1] "txt"  "html" "txt"
```

Location of a substring

In some circumstances, it is necessary to determine the location within a string for the occurrence of a substring. For example, it might be necessary to search a set of filenames to determine whether they contain a match for a predetermined parameter. The command to return the location of a substring is the `regexp` command. This command has many options, and it is explored in more detail in the following section. Here, we use it in its most basic form to determine the location of a substring.

Using the definition of the vector, urls, as an example, we may wish to find the location of the colons in the URLs. The colons are the delimiter between the protocol and the host name, and we cannot assume it will always be in the same position:

```
> colons <- regexpr(":",urls)
> colons
[1] 6 6 5 5
attr(,"match.length")
[1] 1 1 1 1
```

```
attr(,"useBytes")
[1] TRUE
> colons[2]
[1] 6
> colons[3]
[1] 5
```

Note that the assumed position of the first character is one and not zero.

Extracting or changing a substring

There are two commands available to change a substring within a string. The two commands are `substr` and `substring`, and their arguments are identical. The `substring` command is compatible with S, but we focus on the R command `substr`. The command has two forms. One form can be used to extract a substring, and the other form can be used to change the value of a substring.

First, we examine the option to extract a substring. The command takes a string, the location of the start of the substring, and the location of the end of the substring. Making use of the previous example, we now use the `urls` vector defined at the start of the chapter and determine the protocol for each URL:

```
> protocols <- substr(urls,1,colons-1)
> protocols
[1] "https" "https" "http"  "http"
```

A substring can be replaced by combining the `substr` command and the assignment operator. Unfortunately, the length of the string inserted must be the same length as the string being replaced, which can return nonintuitive results. Here, we replace each of the protocols in the `urls` vector with a `mailto` protocol:

```
> colons <- regexpr(":",urls)
> mailto <- urls
> substr(mailto,1,colons-1) <- c("mailto","mailto","mailto")
> mailto
[1] "mailt://duckduckgo.com?q=Johann+Carl+Friedrich+Gauss"
[2] "mailt://search.yahoo.com/search?p=Jean+Baptiste+Joseph+Fourier"
[3] "mail://www.bing.com/search?q=Isaac+Newton"
[4] "mail://www.google.com/search?q=Brahmagupta"
```

Note that the string "http" has fewer characters than the string "mailto," and the command has truncated the new string that is substituted into the original string.

Transforming the case

In some analyses, the case of a letter may not be considered important. In these situations, it may be necessary to convert the case of a string. The `tolower` and `toupper` commands can be used to ensure that a string is in the expected form:

```
> tolower(urls[1])
[1] "https://duckduckgo.com?q=johann+carl+friedrich+gauss"
> toupper(urls[2])
[1] "HTTPS://SEARCH.YAHOO.COM/SEARCH?P=JEAN+BAPTISTE+JOSEPH+FOURIER"
```

An additional command, `chartr`, enables more fine-grained control of character replacement. The idea is that there are some characters in the original string that we want to replace, and we know what the replacement characters are. For example, going back to the `urls` vector defined previously, we may want to replace the occurrences of = with a # character to delimit the end of the URL and the start of the argument list. Suppose we also want to replace the + characters with spaces. We can do so by using the `chartr` command, where the first argument is a string whose character elements will be changed, the second argument is a string that contains the replacement characters, and the third argument is the string to change:

```
> > chartr("=+","# ",urls)
[1] "https://duckduckgo.com?q#Johann Carl Friedrich Gauss"
[2] "https://search.yahoo.com/search?p#Jean Baptiste Joseph Fourier"
[3] "http://www.bing.com/search?q#Isaac Newton"
[4] "http://www.google.com/search?q#Brahmagupta"
```

Splitting strings

A string can be divided into multiple parts using the `strsplit` command. This is useful if you have data in a predefined format and wish to divide the strings into component pieces for a separate analysis. Using the `urls` vector defined earlier, we may wish to divide each URL into its protocol and the rest of the information:

```
> splitURL <- strsplit(urls,":")
> splitURL
[[1]]
[1] "https"
[2] "//duckduckgo.com?q=Johann+Carl+Friedrich+Gauss"

[[2]]
[1] "https"
[2] "//search.yahoo.com/search?p=Jean+Baptiste+Joseph+Fourier"
```

```
[[3]]
[1] "http"
[2] "//www.bing.com/search?q=Isaac+Newton"

[[4]]
[1] "http"
[2] "//www.google.com/search?q=Brahmagupta"

> splitURL[[1]]
[1] "https"
[2] "//duckduckgo.com?q=Johann+Carl+Friedrich+Gauss"
> splitURL[[1]][2]
[1] "//duckduckgo.com?q=Johann+Carl+Friedrich+Gauss"
```

Note that it returns a list, and each entry in the list is a vector of strings that have been split.

Creating formatted strings

The `sprintf` function allows you to take a combination of objects and express them as a formatted string. The `paste`, `format`, and `print` commands have been examined in *Chapter 3, Saving Data and Printing Results*, and those functions can be used to accomplish similar results. The primary difference is that the `sprintf` function acts like the C language's `sprintf` function. For example, suppose we have a loop that performs an analysis on the text found at each of the URLs found in the `urls` vector defined earlier. As part of the analysis, we may have the result of a calculation stored in a variable and wish to use that number in the title for a graph. In the following example, we simply set the value, though, to keep the example more streamlined:

```
> n <- 1
> calculation <- 123.0
> theTitle <- sprintf("URL: %s, Count=%d",urls[n],calculation)
> theTitle
[1] "URL: https://duckduckgo.com?q=Johann+Carl+Friedrich+Gauss,
Count=123"
```

The `%s` characters refer to a string in the argument list, and `%d` refers to an integer next in the argument list. These definitions follow the same specification as the C language definition of `sprintf`.

Regular expressions

The commands examined in the previous section lack flexibility, but they are straightforward in their implementation. The use of regular expressions, on the other hand, offers a more elegant approach in many circumstances, but they can be more complex. We briefly examine a few commands that allow string manipulations via regular expressions, and we assume that you are familiar with regular expressions. To get more information about regular expressions in R you can use the `help(regular expression)` command.

In this section, we will focus on the `gregexpr` and `gsub` commands. There are a number of other commands that are listed when you enter the `help(gregexpr)` command. Also, the commands have a number of options, but we will only examine their most basic forms. As a quick note, the pattern submitted to the `grep` command discussed earlier can also be a regular expression.

The `gregexpr` command is a general command that returns the number of results with respect to the regular expression. In particular, it will return the location of a match, whether or not a match was found, and the number of characters in `match`. The first argument to the function is a pattern and then the strings to match. The function returns a list that has information about `match`. In the following example, we examine the results of searching for the = delimiter in the first entry in our `urls` vector defined earlier:

```
> loc <- gregexpr("=",urls[[1]])
> loc
[[1]]
[1] 25
attr(,"match.length")
[1] 1
attr(,"useBytes")
[1] TRUE

> loc[[1]][1]
[1] 25
```

Note that the function returns a list. Since the use of a single brace returns another list, we use the double braces to ensure that we return the element within the list as a vector.

The `sub` command can be used to replace all occurrences of a pattern within a string. This function takes three arguments, the pattern, the replacement string, and the strings that are used to perform the operation:

```
> sub("\\?.*$","",urls)
[1] "https://duckduckgo.com"        "https://search.yahoo.com/search"
[3] "http://www.bing.com/search"    "http://www.google.com/search"
```

Note that two backslashes must be used in the previous example. The first backslash is used to indicate that the next character is a symbol to be interpreted, and if a second backslash is used, then it means to interpret the pair as a single backslash.

Summary

In this chapter, we have explored a variety of ways to manipulate string variables. Two broad categories have been explored. The first set of functions provide a number of functions with a narrow range of functionality. These functions are relatively straightforward but must often be used together to accomplish complex tasks. The second set of functions make use of regular expressions, and they can be used to accomplish a complex set of tasks using a small number of steps.

In the next chapter, we move on to the topic of working with variables associated with time. This includes translating strings into R's built-in time types, and it also includes the kind of operations that can be performed on time variables.

6
Converting and Defining Time Variables

This chapter provides a broad overview of the ways to convert and store time variables. This is a mundane topic, but it is common to have data that contains date and time information in a wide variety of forms. There are roughly three parts in this chapter:

- **Converting strings to time data types**: This section gives you an introduction to the methods available to take a time stamp in text format and convert it into one of R's internal time formats

- **Converting time data types to strings**: This section gives you an introduction to the methods available to take a time data type and convert it to a string so that it can be saved to a file in a standard format

- **Operations on time data types**: This section gives you an overview of the methods and techniques used to perform basic arithmetic on time data types

Introduction and assumptions

Date and time formations are often saved as part of the information within a dataset. Converting the information into a date or time variable is one of the less exciting chores to perform, and it is something that requires a great deal of care. In this chapter, we will discuss the ways of transforming strings and data types and demonstrate how to perform basic arithmetic operations. It is important to note that working with time and date data occurs in a number of different contexts, and there are a number of different libraries, such as chron, lubridate, and date, to help you work with time and data variables.

Our focus here, though, is on R's built-in functions used to work with time and date data. It is important to note that the commands explored here can be sensitive to small variations within a data file, and you should always double check your work especially with respect to time data. It can be a tedious task, but it is important to make sure that the data is correct. If you commonly work with time data, you should read the details found using the help(DateTimeClasses) command.

Another complication is that time zones can change, and the general practices associated with time data can change. For example, new time zones can be changed, created, or removed, or a region can change its time zone. You should always ensure that your practices associated with time data are consistent with the practice used to generate the data that you have.

Converting strings to time data types

The first task to examine is to take a string and convert it to each of the internal time formats. The strptime command will take a string and convert it to a POSIXlt time variable. If you wish to convert a string to a POSIXct data type, you can cast the result of strptime using the as.POSIXct command. We first focus on converting a string to a POSIXlt data type and provide an example at the end of this section to be converted to a POSIXct data type.

To convert a string to a time data type, the format for the string must be specified, and the formatting options must conform to the ISO C99/POSIX standard. The string includes a sequence of literal characters and a partial list of conversion substrings, which is given in *Table 1*. For example, the %Y-%m-%d %H:%M:%S string indicates that the date should look like *2014-05-14 09:54:10* when referring to May 14, 2014 at 9:54 in the morning. A string is assumed to include any number of predefined strings. Anything else is considered to be a literal character that must appear exactly as it appears in the format string.

Once the format string has been specified, the strptime command can be used to convert a string into the POSIXlt data type. The arguments for the command are the strings to convert, followed by the format string:

```
> theTime <- c("08:30:00 1867-07-01","18:15:00 1864-10-27")
> converted <- strptime(theTime,"%H:%M:%S %Y-%m-%d")
> converted
[1] "1867-07-01 08:30:00" "1864-10-27 18:15:00"
> typeof(converted[1])
[1] "list"
> converted[1]-converted[2]
Time difference of 976.5938 days
```

The command also accepts an optional time zone option, as follows:

```
> theTime <- c("08:30:00 1867-07-01","18:15:00 1864-10-27")
> converted <- strptime(theTime,"%H:%M:%S %Y-%m-%d", +
                        tz="Canada/Eastern")
> converted
[1] "1867-07-01 08:30:00 EST" "1864-10-27 18:15:00 EST"
> converted[1]-converted[2]
Time difference of 976.5938 days
```

The results returned by the strptime command are of the POSIXlt data type. They can be converted using the as.POSIXct command:

```
> theTime <- c("08:30:00 1867-07-01","18:15:00 1864-10-27")
> converted <- strptime(theTime,"%H:%M:%S %Y-%m-%d",tz="Canada/
Eastern")
> converted
[1] "1867-07-01 08:30:00 EST" "1864-10-27 18:15:00 EST"
> typeof(converted[1])
[1] "list"
> otherTime <- as.POSIXct(converted)
> otherTime
[1] "1867-07-01 08:30:00 EST" "1864-10-27 18:15:00 EST"
> typeof(otherTime[1])
[1] "double"
> cat(otherTime[1],"\n")
-3234681000
```

Note that when the date variables are printed, they are converted to a human-readable format. This is convenient, but it can hide the underlying data type. Again, you should be careful about variables that have a time data type since it is easy to lose track of how the R environment is actually treating the values.

Another important concern that you should be wary of is that the strptime command will not give a visible indication when an error occurs. It will return NA in place of each error, as follows:

```
> aTime <- c("2014-05-05 08:00:00","2014/05/05 08:00:00")
> internal <- strptime(aTime,"%Y/%m/%d %H:%M:%S")
> internal
[1] NA                     "2014-05-05 08:00:00"
> is.na(internal)
[1]  TRUE FALSE
```

Another way to save the date and time information in a file is to specify the date and time in one column. If the information from the file is stored as a data frame, then a new column can be added that contains the information saved in an internal format:

```
> fileInfo <- data.frame(time=c("2014-01-01 00:00:00",
+ "2013-12-31 23:59:50","2013-12-31 23:55:12"),
+ happiness=c(1.0,0.9,0.8))
> fileInfo
                  time happiness
1 2014-01-01 00:00:00       1.0
2 2013-12-31 23:59:50       0.9
3 2013-12-31 23:55:12       0.8
> fileInfo$internalTime <- strptime(fileInfo$time,"%Y-%m-%d %H:%M:%S")
> fileInfo
                  time happiness          internalTime
1 2014-01-01 00:00:00       1.0 2014-01-01 00:00:00
2 2013-12-31 23:59:50       0.9 2013-12-31 23:59:50
3 2013-12-31 23:55:12       0.8 2013-12-31 23:55:12
> summary(fileInfo)
         time          happiness        internalTime
 2013-12-31 23:55:12:1  Min.   :0.80  Min.   :2013-12-31 23:55:12
 2013-12-31 23:59:50:1  1st Qu.:0.85  1st Qu.:2013-12-31 23:57:31
 2014-01-01 00:00:00:1  Median :0.90  Median :2013-12-31 23:59:50
                        Mean   :0.90  Mean   :2013-12-31 23:58:20
                        3rd Qu.:0.95  3rd Qu.:2013-12-31 23:59:55
                        Max.   :1.00  Max.   :2014-01-01 00:00:00
```

The various commands used to convert a string to a time or date variable have a large variety of options. These options can be found with R using the `help(trptime)` command. A list of the options can also be found in the following table:

Format string	Meaning	Format string	Meaning
%a	Abbreviation for the name of the day of the week	%p	Indicator for "A.M." or "P.M."
%A	Full name of the day of the week	%S	Seconds as a number (00-61); leap seconds are allowed
%b	Abbreviation for the name of the month	%U	Weak of the year as a number (00-53)
%B	Full name of the month	%w	Weekday as a number (0=Sunday, 1=Monday, ..., 6=Saturday)

Format string	Meaning	Format string	Meaning
`%c`	The date and time in the format `%a %b %e %H:%M:%S %Y`	`%x`	Date in the form `"%y/%m/%d"`
`%d`	Day of the month as a number (01 through 31)	`%X`	Time in the format `"%H:%M:%S"`
`%H`	Hours as a number (00-23); note that `24` is allowed as an exception when used as 24:00:00	`%y`	Year as two digits ("00-99"), and 00-68 refer to the 2000s while 69-99 refer to the 1900s
`%I`	Hours in 12 hour format as a number (01-12)	`%Y`	Year as four digits (>=*1582*)
`%j`	Day of the year as a number (001-366)	`%z`	Offset from UTC (-0500 is five hours behind UTC)
`%m`	Month as a number (01-12)	`%Z`	Time zone as a string (only available for converting time to a string)
`%M`	Minute as a number (00-59)		

Table 1 – characters used to define the formats of dates

More options are available and can be viewed using the `help(strftime)` command within the R environment.

Converting time data types to strings

A date and time variable can be converted to a string using the `strftime` command. Its format is similar to the `strptime` command, except it has one additional option to determine whether or not to include time zone information in the resulting string. The command is a convenience function, and it calls either the `format.POSIXlt` or `format.POSIXct` command depending on the data type of the time variable. We focus on the `strftime` command because it is familiar to people from a wider variety of programming experiences.

The `strftime` command requires a time variable and a format. It returns a string in the given format (some format options are given in *Table 1*):

```
> theTime <- c("08:30:00 1867-07-01","18:15:00 1864-10-27")
> converted <- strptime(theTime,"%H:%M:%S %Y-%m-%d",
+ tz="Canada/Eastern")
> converted
[1] "1867-07-01 08:30:00 EST" "1864-10-27 18:15:00 EST"
```

```
> typeof(converted)
[1] "list"
> backAgain <- strftime(converted,"%j - %B")
> backAgain
[1] "182 - July"     "301 - October"
> typeof(backAgain[1])
[1] "character"
```

Operations on time data types

A variety of arithmetic operations are available for the time data types, and you should be especially wary when performing any operations. The units that are returned can vary depending on the context. It is extremely easy to lose track of the units and make a spurious comparison. In this section, I'll introduce some of the basic operations and then discuss the `difftime` command. It is possible to perform any operation without the `difftime` command, but the command has an important advantage: it allows you to explicitly define the units.

When you perform simple arithmetic on time data types, it acts in the way you might expect:

```
> earlier <- strptime("2014-01-01 00:00:00","%Y-%m-%d %H:%M:%S")
> later <- strptime("2014-01-02 00:00:00","%Y-%m-%d %H:%M:%S")
> later-earlier
Time difference of 1 days
> timeDiff <- later-earlier
> timeDiff
Time difference of 1 days
> as.double(timeDiff)
[1] 1
> earlier+timeDiff
[1] "2014-01-02 EST"
```

Note that in the previous example, the units used are given in days. One small change, though, results in a different kind of result:

```
> earlier <- strptime("2014-01-01 00:00:00","%Y-%m-%d %H:%M:%S")
> later <- strptime("2014-01-01 12:00:00","%Y-%m-%d %H:%M:%S")
> later-earlier
Time difference of 12 hours
> timeDiff <- later-earlier
> timeDiff
Time difference of 12 hours
> as.double(timeDiff)
[1] 12
```

The R environment will keep track of the difference and its units. If you look at the difftime variable in the previous example, it contains information about what it means:

```
> attributes(timeDiff)
$units
[1] "hours"

$class
[1] "difftime"

> attr(timeDiff,"units")
[1] "hours"
```

You can specify the units by casting the result as a numeric value and providing the units to use:

```
> earlier <- strptime("2014-01-01 00:00:00","%Y-%m-%d %H:%M:%S")
> later <- strptime("2014-01-01 12:00:00","%Y-%m-%d %H:%M:%S")
> timeDiff <- later-earlier
> timeDiff
Time difference of 12 hours
> as.numeric(timeDiff,units="weeks")
[1] 0.07142857
> as.numeric(timeDiff,units="secs")
[1] 43200
```

Because of potential ambiguities, it is usually advantageous to use the difftime command. The difftime command offers a wide range of options, and you should carefully read its help page, help(difftime), to see the options and details. In its most basic use, you can find the difference between two times, and you can specify what units to use:

```
> earlier <- strptime("2014-01-01 00:00:00","%Y-%m-%d %H:%M:%S")
> later <- strptime("2014-01-01 12:00:00","%Y-%m-%d %H:%M:%S")
> timeDiff <- difftime(later,earlier,units="sec")
> timeDiff
Time difference of 43200 secs
> timeDiff <- difftime(later,earlier,units="day")
> timeDiff
Time difference of 0.5 days
```

The units that are available are auto, secs, mins, hours, days, or weeks.

One final note; the `difftime` data type offers a convenient way to perform some time arithmetic options. The `as.difftime` command can be used to specify a time interval, and you can specify the units, so it is more likely that the results are consistent with your expectations:

```
> later <- strptime("2014-01-01 12:00:00","%Y-%m-%d %H:%M:%S")
> oneHour = as.difftime(1,units="hours")
> later+oneHour
[1] "2014-01-01 13:00:00 EST"
```

Summary

A broad overview of the options available to convert between strings and the two time data types was given in this chapter. The `strptime` command is used to convert a string into a `POSIXlt` variable. The `strftime` command is used to convert a time data type into a string. Finally, the basic operators used to perform arithmetic operations between two time variables was discussed, with an emphasis on using the `difftime` command. We also explored the use of the `difftime` data type.

7
Basic Programming

In the previous chapters, we explored the basic aspects of how R stores information and the different ways to organize information. We will now explore the way that operations can be defined and executed, and write a program in R. The ability to create algorithms that combine functions to complete complicated tasks is one of R's best features. We continue the exploration of programming in the next two chapters and focus on object-oriented approaches. This chapter is divided into four parts:

- **Conditional execution**: In this section, we will introduce if-then-else blocks and discuss logical operators

- **Loop constructs**: In this section, we will explore three different ways to implement loops

- **Functions**: In this section, we will discuss how to define functions in R and explore some of the important considerations associated with functions

- **Script execution**: In this section, we will discuss how to execute a set of commands that have been saved in a file

Conditional execution

The first control construct examined is the `if` statement. An `if` statement will determine whether or not a code block should be executed, and it has an optional `else` statement. An additional `if` statement can be chained to an `else` statement to create a cascade of options.

In its most basic form, an `if` statement has the following form:

```
if(condition)
    code block
```

The condition can be a logical statement constructed from the operators given in the next table, or it can be a numeric result. If the condition is numeric, then zero is considered to be FALSE, otherwise the statement is TRUE. The code block can either be a single statement or a set of statements enclosed in braces:

```
> # check if 1 is less than 2
> if(1<2)
+     cat("one is smaller than two.\n")
one is smaller than two.
> if(2>1) {
+     cat("But two is bigger yet.\n")
+ }
But two is bigger yet.
```

Note that a comment is included in the previous code. The # character is used to denote a comment. Anything after the # character is ignored.

The if statement can be extended using an else statement. The else statement allows you to specify a code block to execute if the condition does not evaluate to TRUE:

```
> if(1>2) {
+     cat("One is the most biggest number\n")   # Say something wrong
+ } else {
+     cat("One is the loneliest number\n")      # Say something less
wrong
+ }
One is the loneliest number
```

The first thing to note about these examples is that a **Kernighan and Ritchie (K&R)** indentation style is adopted. We adopted the K&R style because the else statement must be on the same line as the closing brace. The second thing to note is that another if statement can be appended to the else statement so that a standard if-then-else block can be constructed:

```
> if(0) {
+     cat("Yes, that is FALSE.\n")
+ } else if (1) {
+     cat("Yes that is TRUE\n")
+ } else {
+     cat("Whatever")
+ }
Yes that is TRUE
```

One potential issue is that R does not have a scalar type and assumes most data types are arranged in vectors. This can lead to potential problems with a logical statement. The first element in the vector is used to decide whether a whole statement is TRUE or FALSE. Fortunately, R will give a warning if the condition evaluates to a vector of length greater than one:

```
> x <- c(1,2)
> if(x < 2) {
+    cat("Oh yes it is\n")
+ }
Oh yes it is
Warning message:
In if (x < 2) { :
   the condition has length > 1 and only the first element will be used
```

This is something to keep in mind when deciding which logical operator to use in an if statement. For example, the | operator will perform a logical OR on all elements of the vectors, but the || operator will only perform a logical OR on the first elements of the vectors:

```
> x <- c(FALSE,FALSE,TRUE)
> y <- c(FALSE,TRUE,TRUE)
> x|y
[1] FALSE   TRUE   TRUE
> x||y
[1] FALSE
```

A variety of logical operators are recognized. Some provide comparisons between all entries in a vector and others are for comparisons only for the first elements in the vectors. A list of the operators is given in the following table:

Operator	Description	Operator	Description
<	Less than (vector)	|	Or (vector)
>	Greater than (vector)	||	Or (first entry only)
<=	Less than or equal (vector)	!	Not (vector)
>=	Greater than or equal (vector)	&	And (vector)
==	Equal to (vector)	&&	And (first entry only)
!=	Not equal to (vector)	xor(a,b)	Exclusive or (vector)

Table 1 – The logical operators including comparison operators

Loop constructs

Another important programming task is to create a set of instructions that can be repeated in a structured way. There are three loop constructs in R: for, while, and repeat loops. We will explore each of these loop constructs and discuss the break and next commands, which can control how the instructions within a loop's code block are executed. More details are available using the help(Control) command.

The for loop

A for loop takes a vector, and it repeats a block of code for each value in the vector. The syntax is as follows:

```
for(var in vector)
   code block
```

The for loop repeats a set of instructions for every value within a vector in the appropriate order. It can be memory intensive if you need to repeat the loop a lot of times and the vector is not already stored in the workspace. An example of a simple for loop is given here:

```
> for(lupe in seq(1,2,by=0.33))
+ {
+     cat("The value of lupe is ",lupe,"\n")
+ }
The value of lupe is  1
The value of lupe is  1.33
The value of lupe is  1.66
The value of lupe is  1.99
```

The while loop

A while loop will execute a code block as long as a given expression is true. The syntax is as follows:

```
while(condition)
   code block
```

They are often used when the number of iterations is not known in advance and the loop is repeated until some criteria is met. Also, the `while` loop has some advantages over the `for` loop. It can be more efficient, especially with respect to memory, and it is more flexible (RMemory, Please refer to RMemory: Hadley Wickham, memory, 2014, `http://adv-r.had.co.nz/memory.html` for more information on this topic). For example, instead of constructing a large vector to iterate over its elements, a single index can be used. On the down side, it can be harder to read, and it can require a little more care when writing the code. An example is given here:

```
> lupe <- 1.0;
> while(lupe <= 2.0)
+ {
+     cat("The value of lupe is ",lupe,"\n")
+     lupe <- lupe + 0.33
+ }
The value of lupe is  1
The value of lupe is  1.33
The value of lupe is  1.66
The value of lupe is  1.99
```

The repeat loop

A `repeat` loop is used to denote a block of code that will be repeatedly executed until an explicit breakout of the block is executed. The primary advantage of the `repeat` loop is that the start of the code block will always be executed. One disadvantage is that it can be difficult to read. The syntax is relatively simple:

```
repeat
    code block
```

You must use a `break` command to tell R to exit the code block. The `break` command is described in the next subsection in more detail. An example of a `repeat` loop is given in the following example, and it is a brief example of simulation of a random walk in the complex plane:

```
positions    <- complex(0) # Initialize the history of positions
currentPos   <- 0.0+0.0i   # Start at the origin
NUMBERSTEPS  <- 50         # Number of steps to take
angleFacing  <- 0.0        # direction it is facing
stdDev       <- 1.0        # std dev. of the change in the angle

step <- as.integer(0)
repeat
    {
        ## Update the current time step
```

```
        step <- step + as.integer(1)

        ## Check to see if it is time to stop
        if(step>MAXNUMBER)
            break

        ## Add new people to the line and update the length
        angle <- angle + rnorm(1,0.0,stdDev)
        currentPos <- currentPos + exp(angle*1.0i)
        positions  <- c(positions,currentPos)


    }
plot(Re(positions),Im(positions),type="l")
```

Break and next statements

The break and next statements are used to influence which part of the code in the current loop will be executed. The break statement will move to the very end of the current block and it will stop the execution of the loop. The next statement will act as if the end of the code block was reached and start over at the beginning of the code block to begin the next iteration.

As a demonstration, we build on the simulation of the random walk in the previous example. We alter the model by placing a restriction on the position. If a step moves to the left-hand part of the plane, it is ignored:

```
    positions    <- complex(0) # Initialize the history of positions
    currentPos   <- 0.0+0.0i   # Start at the origin
    NUMBERSTEPS <- 50          # Number of steps to take
    angleFacing  <- 0.0        # direction it is facing
    stdDev       <- 1.0        # std dev. of the change in the angle


step <- as.integer(0)
repeat
    {
        ## Add new people to the line and update the length
        newAngle     <- angle + rnorm(1,0.0,stdDev)
        proposedStep <- currentPos + exp(newAngle*1.0i)
        if(Re(proposedStep) < 0.0)
            next   # Ignore this step. It moves to neg. real parts

        ## update the position
        angle       <- newAngle
        currentPos <- proposedStep
```

```
    positions  <- c(positions,currentPos)

    ## Update the current time step
    step <- step + as.integer(1)

    ## Check to see if it is time to stop
    if(step>MAXNUMBER)
        break
}
plot(Re(positions),Im(positions),type="l")
```

Functions

Another common programming task is to define a function or subroutine that can be executed with a single call. Defining and using functions can be complicated because of the technical details associated with working with variables that exist in different contexts but may have the same name. Another problem that arises is that everything in R is an object. Up to this point, we have quietly ignored this issue, but it is a technical issue that we must now consider. In this section, we will first demonstrate how to define a function. We will then discuss the details about how arguments are passed to a function. Finally, we discuss the technical details of how R determines what a variable name means.

Before we get into those details, we will provide a note about how R keeps track of functions. When we define a variable, R treats that variable as an object that can be accessed using the name we assign to the variable. Likewise, when you define a new function, it is assigned a variable name, and the variable is an object.

Defining a function

As previously mentioned, when a function is defined, it is assigned to an object and treated like any other variable. The format for a function definition is as follows:

```
function (arg1, arg2, ... )
    code block
```

This will create an object, and you must assign a variable name to the object. If you print out the value of the variable, it will print out the definition of the function. In the following example, suppose we need a function used to simulate a random walk in the complex plane. The function takes the current position and adds a unit step in a random direction:

```
> updatePosition <- function(currentPos)
+ {
+       newDirection <- exp(1i*runif(1,0.0,2.0*pi))
+       currentPos + newDirection
+ }
>
> updatePosition(0.0)
[1] 0.9919473-0.1266517i
> updatePosition
function(currentPos)
{
    newDirection <- exp(1i*runif(1,0.0,2.0*pi))
    currentPos + newDirection
}
```

One oddity associated with functions is that the value it returns is the last expression evaluated within the code block.

There are times when you want a function to perform operations that impact more than one variable. In such cases, you may need to return a combination of results. For difficult results that cannot be expressed as a vector, you can return the result as a list. In the following example, we extend the previous example and wish to return the new position as well as the updated direction of movement:

```
> updatePosition <- function(currentPos,angle,stdDev)
+ {
+       angle <- angle + rnorm(1,0,stdDev)
+       list(newPos=currentPos + exp(angle*1.0i),
+           newAngle=angle)
+ }
>
> pos <- updatePosition(2.0,0.0,1.0)
> pos
$newPos
[1] 2.986467+0.163962i

$newAngle
[1] 0.164706
```

```
> pos$newPos
[1] 2.986467+0.163962i
```

It is possible to explicitly specify the value returned by a function using the `return` command. The `return` command takes at most one argument. The command will exit the function and return the value given in the argument if it exists. In the following example, we build on our example of a random walk in the complex plane. Here, we assume that the left-hand side of the plane is not reachable, and if the real part of a step is negative, then the step moves in the opposite direction:

```
> updatePosition <- function(currentPos,angle,stdDev)
+ {
+      angle <- angle + rnorm(1,0.0,stdDev)
+      newStep <- exp(angle*1.0i)
+      if(Re(currentPos + newStep)<0.0)
+          {
+                  # This would be a move in the left hand part of the
+                  # plane.
+                  # Move in the opposite direction.
+                  return(list(newPos=currentPos - newStep,
+                          newAngle=angle+pi))
+          }
+      # All is good. Accept this move.
+      return(list(newPos=currentPos + newStep,
+                  angle=angle))
+ }
>
> pos <- updatePosition(-0.1+2i,0.0,1.0)
> pos$newPos
[1] 0.459425+2.828881i
```

Arguments to functions

We have discussed how to define a new function and briefly discussed how to pass arguments to a function. We now focus on some details about passing arguments to a function. First, we note that the arguments that are passed to a function are passed as values and not references. Any changes you make to an argument do not impact the variable outside the function. In the following example, we go back to our function to update the position for a random walk in the complex plane. We pass the angle to the function that is changed within the function but not outside of the function:

```
> updatePosition <- function(currentPos,angle,stdDev)
+ {
+      angle <- angle + rnorm(1,0.0,stdDev)
```

```
+        currentPos + exp(1i*angle)
+ }
>
> angle <- 0.0
> updatePosition(1+2i,angle,1.0)
[1]  0.250178+2.661639i
> angle
[1]  0
```

Another important point is that you can provide default values for some arguments. If a default value is given for a variable, then it is not required while calling the function:

```
> updatePosition <- function(currentPos,angle=0.0)
+ {
+       print(noquote(paste("Angle is ",angle)))
+       angle <- angle + runif(1,0.0,2.0*pi)
+       currentPos + exp(1i*angle)
+ }
>
> updatePosition(1+2i)
[1] Angle is   0
[1]  0.091507+2.417901i
> updatePosition(1+2i,pi)
[1] Angle is   3.14159265358979
[1]  0.029198+2.239884i
```

There are circumstances in which you might wish to check whether a particular argument has been specified when the function is called. This can be done using the `missing` command. In the next example, we test whether or not the angle is provided:

```
> updatePosition <- function(currentPos,angle=0.0)
+ {
+       if(missing(angle))
+           {
+               warning("Using the default drift: ",angle)
+           }
+       angle <- angle + runif(1,0.0,2.0*pi)
+       currentPos + exp(1i*angle)
+ }
>
> updatePosition(1+2i)
[1]  0.552725+1.105604i
```

```
Warning message:
In updatePosition(1 + (0+2i)) : Using the default drift: 0
> updatePosition(1+2i,pi)
[1] 0.054151+1.675394i
```

Note that the `warning` command was used to print out a message. When executing a function, it may be beneficial to print a warning or to stop the execution of the function due to an error condition. The `stop` and `warning` commands can be used for these situations. The `warning` command prints out a warning and continues execution as normal. The `stop` command will print out a message and exit the function:

```
> updatePosition <- function(currentPos,angle=0.0)
+ {
+     if(abs(angle) > 2.0*pi)
+         {
+             stop("I arbitrarily do not like angles that big")
+         }
+     angle <- angle + runif(1,0.0,2.0*pi)
+     currentPos + exp(1i*angle)
+ }
>
> pos1 <- updatePosition(1+2i)
> pos2 <- updatePosition(1+2i,3.0*pi)
Error in updatePosition(1 + (0+2i), 3 * pi) :
  I arbitrarily do not like angles that big
> pos2
Error: object 'pos2' not found
```

Note that in the last line, the `stop` command was called and the function did not return a value. The result is that the variable `pos2` does not exist. Be careful though, as if the variable `pos2` had been previously defined, it would retain its previous value.

In the preceding examples, there is an assumption about the order of the arguments when calling a function. In the previous examples, the arguments are matched according to the order they appear in the function call. You can circumvent this convention by specifying the name when you call the function. The caveat is that R does not require that the name should match exactly, and it will try to match the names using the first characters in the name. If the match is ambiguous, you will get an error message:

```
> matching <- function(argOne,argTwo)
+ {
+     return(paste("I got this: ",argOne,' ',argTwo))
+ }
```

```
> matching(argTwo="second",argOne="First")
[1] "I got this:  First   second"
> matching(argT="2nd",argO="1st")
[1] "I got this:  1st    2nd"
> matching(argT="two",arg="one")
Error in matching(argT = "two", arg = "one") :
  argument 2 matches multiple formal arguments
```

The last issue to discuss is how to limit the potential values that an argument may have. The default values for an argument can be given as a vector of values. If no argument is given, it defaults to the first entry in the vector. If you wish to limit the values to be one of the values in the vector, you can use the `match.arg` function to test the value:

```
> updatePosition <- function(currentPos,angle=0.0,
+                    dist=c("uniform","normal"))
+       {
+           dist <- match.arg(dist)
+           print(dist)
+           # Update position code would go below
+       }
>
> updatePosition(0.0,0.0)
[1] "uniform"
> updatePosition(0.0,0.0,"uniform")
[1] "uniform"
> updatePosition(0.0,0.0,"neither")
Error in match.arg(dist) : 'arg' should be one of "uniform", "normal"
```

Scope

An important question when dealing with a function is how to decide what a symbol means. This idea is referred to as `scope`, and the language used to describe the ideas associated with scope can be confusing. Unfortunately, it is something that needs to be considered, and we try to discuss some of the ideas here. It is also important to note that the details discussed here represent an area in which R is not consistent with the **S_PLUS** language, so be careful about generalizing these ideas. For further information, you can enter the `demo(scoping)` command in the R environment and a brief demonstration of the notion of scope is given. If you enter the `help(environment)` command, you can also find more details.

The basic idea is that R maintains a hierarchy of environments. Each environment has a list of symbols that are associated with that environment. You can create a new environment that is embedded within another environment. The new.env command is used to create an environment. This environment holds its own variables, and variables can be created using the assign command. The values can be obtained using the get command:

```
> envOne <- new.env()
> typeof(envOne)
[1] "environment"
> ls()
[1] "envOne"
> ls(envOne)
character(0)
>
>
> assign("bubba",12,envir=envOne)
> ls()
[1] "envOne"
> ls(envOne)
[1] "bubba"
> envOne$bubba
[1] 12
> get("bubba",envOne)
[1] 12
> bubba
Error: object 'bubba' not found
```

Note that in the preceding example, we used the optional environment argument to the ls command, which specifies which environment to use. The environment is used to guide R in how to interpret the meaning of a symbol. The R environment maintains a path that it uses to search in a particular order to find a symbol. One way to manipulate the path is to use the attach and detach commands. The attach and detach commands have numerous options, but we focus on how to use it with environments. We also provide a warning that using these commands can lead to confusion about the meaning of a symbol, and you should exercise caution when using these commands:

```
> ls()
character(0)
> one <- 2
> ls()
[1] "one"
> envTwo <- new.env()
```

```
> assign("two",3,envir=envTwo)
> two
Error: object 'two' not found
> attach(envTwo)
> ls()
[1] "envTwo" "one"
> two
[1] 3
> detach(envTwo)
> two
Error: object 'two' not found
```

The reason we explore this topic here is that when you define a function, a new environment is created that exists within the function. When you use a symbol within a function, it can be ambiguous as to what it means. If that symbol has been previously defined within the function, then it is treated as a local variable. If that symbol exists in the parent environment, then it is possible to get access to it or change its value. In *Chapter 1, Data Types*, it was briefly noted that the < - operator is used to assign a variable in the local context. The << - operator is used to tell R to first search the parent environment:

```
> one <- 2
> changeOne <- function(a)
+ {
+     one <- a
+     return(one)
+ }
> changeOne(3)
[1] 3
> one
[1] 2
> realyChangeOne <- function(a)
+ {
+     one <<- a
+     return(one)
+ }
> realyChangeOne(3)
[1] 3
> one
[1] 3
```

Again, `<<-` tells R to use the parent of the current environment. That means that if you create a function within a function, the use of the `<<-` operator within the innermost function will look for a variable in the original (outermost) function. This idea is examined in the following example:

```
> market <- function(rutabagas)
+ {
+       money <- 0
+       return(list(
+           numberRutabagas = function()
+           {
+               return(rutabagas)
+           },
+           revenue = function()
+           {
+               return(money)
+           },
+           harvestRutabagas = function(amount)
+           {
+               rutabagas <<- rutabagas + amount
+           },
+           sellRutabagas = function(amount)
+           {
+               if(rutabagas >= amount)
+                   {
+                       rutabagas <<- rutabagas - amount
+                       money <<- money + amount*0.5
+                   }
+               else
+                   {
+                       warning("We do not have that many rutabagas")
+                   }
+               return(rutabagas)
+           }))
+ }
> farmerJoe <- market(20)
> farmerJoe$numberRutabagas()
[1] 20
> farmerJoe$sellRutabagas(6)
[1] 14
> farmerJoe$numberRutabagas()
[1] 14
```

```
Warning message:
In farmerJoe$sellRutabagas(15) : We do not have that many rutabagas
> farmerJoe$harvestRutabagas(10)
> farmerJoe$numberRutabagas()
[1] 24
```

Note that the preceding example gives us our first taste of object-oriented programming. We will explore this in more detail in *Chapter 8, S3 Classes*, and will build on the idea.

Executing scripts

The final topic is how to execute a set of commands that have been saved in a file using the command line in an interactive R session. All of our examples have been contrived, and the reason for this is to try to focus on a specific idea. The real power of R though is the ability to put together a set of commands and have them executed in order. This can be accomplished using the source command.

We need to have a file to execute. We assume that you have the file given here. You can create this file using any editor capable of saving simple text files, and we assume that the name of the file is simpleExecute.R:

```
# File simpleExecute.R
# This is a simple example used to demonstrate the source command.
# This script will prompt the person running it to enter a number,
# and it will find the square root of the number.
# It tests the original
# number to make sure it is positive and prints out an appropriate
# warning message if it is negative.

x <- as.double(readline("What is the value of x? "))      # Read in a
number
cat("I got the number ",format(x,digits=6),".\n")
if(x < 0)
    {
        # The number is negative. What are they thinking?
        print("Why would you give me a negative number?")
        x <- abs(x)
    }

# Find the square root and assign it the variable "y."
y <- sqrt(x)
```

You can execute the file using the source command. One important thing is that the R environment must find it on your local machine. You can either specify the search path or you can specify the current working directory. The easiest way to do this depends on how you are running R, the interface you are using, and your operating system. We assume that you can specify the current working directory (folder), and the file given earlier is in that directory. Once you specify the current working directory, you can execute the commands using the source command, as follows:

```
> source('simpleExecute.R')
What is the value of x? 2.3
I got the number  2.3 .
> source('simpleExecute.R')
What is the value of x? -2.3
I got the number  -2.3 .
[1] "Why would you give me a negative number, jerk?"
> source('simpleExecute.R',echo=TRUE)

> x <- as.double(readline("What is the value of x? "))
What is the value of x? -2.3

> cat("I got the number ",format(x,digits=6),".\n")
I got the number  -2.3 .

> if(x < 0)
+     {
+          print("Why would you give me a negative number, jerk?")
+          x <- abs(x)
+     }
[1] "Why would you give me a negative number, jerk?"

> y <- sqrt(x)
```

The command has a number of options. One option not explored here is the `verbose` option. This is a helpful option for debugging, and you should try to add the `verbose=TRUE` option. An example is omitted because referring to it as verbose is an understatement.

Summary

This chapter introduced basic ideas to specify optional execution of certain commands and the three basic loop constructs. We had to take a side trip to discuss the idea of scope and explore how R finds and interprets the meaning of a variable name. You can combine these ideas to create and implement algorithms and execute commands in a file.

This chapter also includes our first taste of object-oriented programming in the sense of an S3 class. We build on this idea in the next chapter where the S3 class is formally defined. In doing so, we explore how existing functions can be extended to accommodate arguments that include a class that we have constructed.

8
S3 Classes

This is the second chapter in our introduction to programming. In the preceding chapter, we explored the basic control structures that help us to define the code that is executed, and we had our first taste of objects. We will now build on the idea of object-oriented programming, concentrating on s3 classes. There are two approaches, s3 and s4 classes. It is common for some people to use only one exclusively.

This chapter is divided into three parts:

- **Defining classes and methods**: This section will give a general idea of how methods are defined whose function depends on the class name of the primary argument
- **Objects and inheritance**: In this section, we will discuss the way in which objects of a given class can be defined; we will also introduce the idea of inheritance in the context of s3 classes
- **Encapsulation**: In this section, we will discuss the importance of encapsulation with respect to a class and how it is handled within the context of an R class

At first glance, s3 objects do not appear to behave like objects as defined in other languages. The definition is an odd implementation compared to Java or C++. On the plus side, s3 objects are relatively simple and can offer a powerful way to deal with a wide variety of circumstances.

We have seen a variety of data structures as well as functions, and in this chapter, we will see how the class attribute can be used to dictate how a function responds when a list is passed to a function. The idea is that the class attribute for an object is a vector of names, and the vector represents an ordered set of names to search when deciding what action a function should take. We will build on and extend one example throughout this chapter. The idea is that we wish to create a set of classes that can be used to simulate a random variable, which follows a geometric distribution. There will be two classes. The first class is for a fair coin, in which we flip the coin until *heads* is tossed. The second class is for a fair, six-sided die, in which we roll until a *1* is rolled.

Defining classes and methods

The `class` command is similar to other attribute commands, and it can be used to either set or get information about an object's class. An object's class is a vector, and each item in the vector is the name of a class. The first element in the class vector is the object's base class, and it inherits from the other classes as you read from left to right.

We first focus on the situation where an object has a single class and will examine inheritance in the section that follows. The example examined throughout this chapter is used to simulate one experiment that follows a geometric distribution. The idea is that you repeat some experiment and stop when the first success occurs. First, we examine two classes, and we construct a function that will take an action depending on the class name. The first class is used to represent a fair, six-sided die. The die will be rolled, giving an integer between 1 and 6 inclusive, and the experiment stops when a 1 is returned. The second class represents a fair coin. The coin will be flipped returning either an H or a T, and the experiment stops when H is returned.

The two class definitions are illustrated in the following figure. Each class keeps track of the trials, and the results are kept in a vector. The two methods include a method to reset the history, but more will be added when we examine inheritance. In this example, we are not creating methods in the traditional sense but are creating functions that take appropriate action based on the class name of the argument passed to them. Have a look at the following diagram:

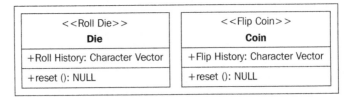

The methods associated with the die and coin classes

First, we define the two classes. Each class is composed of a list, and the class names are set to Die and Coin respectively. (The names are strings that we make up.) Each class consists of a list with a single numeric vector that initially has a length of zero. In each of the following cases, the list is created manually, and a class name is defined. We could have used a vector, but we used a list so that the examples are consistent with the way we extend the classes later:

```
> oneDie <- list(trials=character(0))
> class(oneDie) <- "Die"

> oneCoin <- list(trials=character(0))
> class(oneCoin) <- "Coin"
```

First, we define two sets of functions. The first set of functions resets the history, and the second set performs a single Bernoulli trial. We first focus on a routine to reset and initialize the history, and define a function called reset. The reset function makes use of three different functions. The first uses the UseMethod command, which will tell R to search for the appropriate function to call. The decision is based on the class name of the object passed to it as the first argument. The UseMethod command looks for other functions whose names have the form resetTrial.class_ name, where the class_name suffix must exactly match the name of the class. The exception is the default suffix that is executed if no other function is found:

```
reset <- function(theObject)
    {
        UseMethod("reset",theObject)
        print("Reset the Trials")
    }


reset.default <- function(theObject)
    {
        print("Uh oh, not sure what to do here!\n")
        return(theObject)
    }


reset.Die <- function(theObject)
    {
        theObject$trials <- character(0)
        print("Reset the die\n")
        return(theObject)
    }


reset.Coin <- function(theObject)
```

```
        {
            theObject$trials <- character(0)
            print("Reset the coin\n")
            return(theObject)
        }
```

Note that the functions return the object passed to them. Recall that R passes arguments as values. Any changes you make to the variable are local to the function, so the new value must be returned. We can now call the resetTrial function, and it will decide which function to call, given the argument passed to it. Have a look at the following code:

```
> oneDie$trials = c("3","4","1")
> oneDie$trials
[1] "3" "4" "1"

> oneDie <- reset(oneDie)
  Reset the die

> oneDie
$trials
character(0)

attr(,"class")
[1] "Die"

> oneCoin$trials = c("H","H","T")
> oneCoin <- reset(oneCoin)
Reset the coin

> oneDie$trials
character(0)
> # Look at an example that will fail and use the default function.
> v <- c(1,2,3)
> v <- reset(v)
[1] "Uh oh, not sure what to do here!\n"
> v
[1] 1 2 3
```

Note that the print command after the UseMethod command in the function resetTrial is not executed. When the return function is called, any commands that follow the UseMethod command are not executed.

Defining objects and inheritance

The examples given in the previous section should invoke a twinge of shame for those familiar with object-oriented principles, and you should be assured that I felt appropriately embarrassed to share them. It was done, though, to keep the introduction to S3 classes as simple as possible. One issue is that the two classes are closely related, and the functions include a great deal of repeated code. We will now examine how inheritance can be used to avoid this problem.

In this section, we define a base class, GeometricTrial, and then redefine the routines so that the Die and Coin classes can be derived from the base class. In doing so, we can demonstrate how inheritance is implemented in the context of an S3 class. Additionally, we respect the idea of encapsulation, which is the principle that an object of a given class should update its own elements using methods from within the class. We explore this issue in greater detail in the section that follows.

We will now rethink the whole class structure. The die and the coin are closely related, and the only difference is the result returned from a single trial. We reimagine the classes to take advantage of the commonalities between the coin and the die. The new class structure is shown in the following diagram:

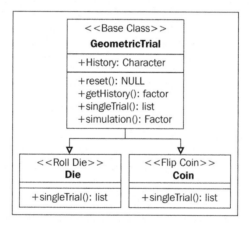

In addition to the change in the classes, we also change the way in which the classes are defined. In this case, we define functions that will act as constructors for each class. Each constructor will use the `class` command to append the name of the class to the object's class attribute. As previously mentioned, the class attribute for an object is a vector. When you call the `UseMethod` command, R will search for a function whose class matches the first element in the vector. If it does not find that function, it looks for a function that matches the second element, and it proceeds until it reaches the last element in the vector. If it does not find anything, it calls the default function. With this in mind, we now examine new definitions of the classes. Rather than manually creating the class, we define functions that will create a list representing the class, append a class name to the `class` attribute, and then return the list. There are three classes, and we will define one function for each class. The first function is used to define a constructor for an object of the `GeometricTrial` class:

```
GeometricTrial <- function()
    {
        # Create the basic data structure - a list that keeps track of
        # a set of trials.

        # Create the basic methods as part of a list to be returned.
        me = list(
            # Define the history to keep track of the trials.
            history = character(0)
            )

        # Define my class identifier and return the list.
        class(me) <- append(class(me),"GeometricTrial")
        return(me)
    }
```

Prior to returning the list, the `append` function is used to add the new class name to the end of the current `class` attribute. This idea is used in classes that are derived from the `GeometricTrial` classes as well. The constructor for the `Die` and `Coin` classes can now be defined, and both constructors explicitly call the constructor for the parent class, perform any actions associated with the current class, and then append the current class name to the `class` attribute:

```
Die <- function()
{
    # Define the object by first calling the constructor for the base
class
    me <- GeometricTrial()
```

```
    # Add the class name to the end of the list of class names
    class(me) <- append(class(me),"Die")
    return(me)
}


Coin <- function()
{
    # Define the object by calling the constructor for the base class
    me <- GeometricTrial()

    # Add the class name to the end of the list of class names
    class(me) <- append(class(me),"Coin")
    return(me)
}
```

The GeometricTrial class includes four methods. The reset method behaves exactly like the reset method discussed in the previous section. The getHistory method is an accessor for a data element and is discussed in the following section. We will now discuss the simulation method, and a discussion on the singleTrial method will follow.

The simulation method is used to simulate a single experiment. The history is first cleared, and the singleTrial method is repeatedly called until a successful result is returned. We first define the base simulation function, the default simulation function, and then the simulation function used by the GeometricTrial class, as follows:

```
simulation <- function(theObject)
    {
        UseMethod("simulation",theObject)
    }


simulation.default <- function(theObject)
    {
        warning("Default simulation method called on unrecognized
object.")
        return(theObject)
    }


## Define a method to run a simulation of a geometric trial.
simulation.GeometricTrial = function(theObject)
    {
        theObject <- reset(theObject)   # Reset the history
```

```
                                                    # before the trial.
        repeat
            {
                ## perform a single trial and add it to the history
                thisTrial  <- singleTrial(theObject)
                theObject <- appendEvent(theObject,thisTrial$result)
                if(thisTrial$success)
                    {
                        break  # The trial resulted in a success. Time
                               # to stop!
                    }
            } # The trial was not a success. Keep going.

        return(theObject)


    }
```

The effort to define a default function may not appear to be a worthwhile endeavor. However, this practice is generally employed to ensure that the system can responsibly react if the methods you define are called by mistake.

The final step is to define the `singleTrial` methods. This method is executed by the child classes, `Die` and `Coin`. Again, the base and default methods are created. In this case, though, there are also methods for each of the three classes. The base function calls the `UseMethod` function, which scrolls through the `class` attribute for the first function to call. We use a method for the `GeometricTrial` class to demonstrate the order of the calls as well as the `NextMethod` function. The `NextMethod` function continues the search in the class attribute and will call the next function based on the class names that follow the current class:

```
singleTrial.default = function(theObject)
    {
        ## Just generate a default success
        warning("Unrecognized object found for the singleTrial
method")
        return(list(result="1",success=TRUE))
    }

singleTrial.GeometricTrial = function(theObject)
    {
        NextMethod("singleTrial",theObject)
    }

singleTrial.Coin = function(theObject)
```

```
    {
        ## Perform a single coin flip
        value <- as.character(
            cut(as.integer(1+trunc(runif(1,0,2))),c(0,1,2),labels=c("
H","T")))
        return(list(result=value,success=(value=="H")))
    }

singleTrial.Die = function(theObject)
    {
        ## Perform a single die roll
        value <- as.integer(1+trunc(runif(1,0,6)))
        return(list(result=value,success=(value==1)))
    }
```

With these methods defined and the `getHistory` method defined in the following section, the class will be complete. Objects of the `Coin` and `Die` class can be created, and simulations can be executed, as follows:

```
> coin <- Coin()
> coin <- simulation(coin)
> getHistory(coin)
[1] H
Levels: H
> coin <- simulation(coin)
> getHistory(coin)
[1] T T H
Levels: H T
>
> die <- Die()
> die <- simulation(die)
> getHistory(die)
[1] 1
Levels: 1
> die <- simulation(die)
> getHistory(die)
[1] 6 5 5 6 2 1
Levels: 1 2 5 6
```

Encapsulation

The final method for the `getHistory` class will now be defined. It is defined in a separate section to stress an important point. An S3 object is generally a basic data structure, such as a vector or a list that has an additional class attribute defined. The functions that are defined for the class react to the `class` attribute in a predictable way.

One side effect is that every element of an object from a given class is public data. The elements contained within an object can always be accessed. The result is that when programming in R, we must take extra steps to maintain discipline with respect to accessing the data elements maintained by an object. Code that directly accesses data elements within an object may work when first written, but any change to the class constructor risks breaking code in the other methods defined for a class.

With respect to our previous example, we have an accessor, the `getHistory` method. If we have an object, called `oneDie`, from the `Die` class, we can easily get the history using `oneDie$history`. If we later decide to change the data structure used to store the history, then any code directly accessing this variable is likely to fail.

Instead, we write an accessor method, `getHistory`, which is designed to return a vector that has the history in the form of a vector of factors. It is important to maintain discipline and only use this method to get a copy of the history. Have a look at the following code:

```
getHistory <- function(theObject)
    {
        UseMethod("getHistory",theObject)
    }


getHistory.default <- function(theObject)
    {
        return(factor()) # Just return an empty vector of factors
    }


getHistory.GeometricTrial <- function(theObject)
    {
        return(as.factor(theObject$history))
    }
```

A final note

There is one final note to share about S3 classes. If you have used R, you most likely have used them. Many functions are defined to react according to the class name of their first argument. Have a look at the following diagram:

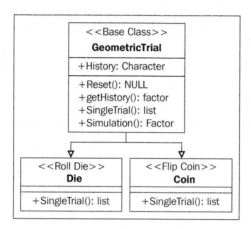

A common example of this is the `plot` command. If you type the `plot` command without arguments, you can see its definition, as follows:

```
> plot
function (x, y, ...)
UseMethod("plot")
<bytecode: 0x32fdd50>
<environment: namespace:graphics>
>
```

The `plot` command will react differently depending on what kind of object you passed to it. If you wish to see what classes the `plot` command can handle, you can use the `methods` command to list them:

```
> methods(plot)
 [1] plot.HoltWinters*    plot.TukeyHSD*        plot.acf*
 [4] plot.data.frame*     plot.decomposed.ts*   plot.default
 [7] plot.dendrogram*     plot.density*         plot.ecdf
[10] plot.factor*         plot.formula*         plot.function
[13] plot.hclust*         plot.histogram*       plot.isoreg*
[16] plot.lm*             plot.medpolish*       plot.mlm*
[19] plot.ppr*            plot.prcomp*          plot.princomp*
[22] plot.profile.nls*    plot.spec*            plot.stepfun
```

```
[25] plot.stl*           plot.table*          plot.ts
[28] plot.tskernel*

    Non-visible functions are asterisked
>
```

One of the greatest advantages of the S3 class definition is that it is simple to build on what is already available. In the example from the previous section, I would like to have the `plot` command react appropriately according to whether or not I pass it a class of the type `Die` or `Coin`. Assuming that I have the previous classes, `Die` and `Coin`, defined, I merely have to define two new plot functions, as follows:

```
> plot.Die <- function(theDie,theTitle)
+     {
+          plot(theDie$getHistory(),
+              xlab="Value After A Die Roll",ylab="Frequency",
+              main=theTitle)
+     }
>
> plot.Coin <- function(theCoin,theTitle)
+     {
+          plot(theCoin$getHistory(),
+              xlab="Value After Coin Flip",ylab="Frequency",
+              main=theTitle)
+     }
> plot(aCoin,"This Here Trial")
> plot(aDie,"A More Better Trial")
```

It is common to use this idea to extend a number of commands. Some common examples include the `print` and the `format` functions.

Summary

We have explored how to create S3 classes, and we did so in the context of two examples. The first example focused on how to define functions that will react based on the class name of the first argument given to the function. The first example did not make full use of basic object-oriented principles, as it is an attempt to simply introduce the idea of S3 classes. The second example extended the first example to provide a simple example of how inheritance is implemented. It demonstrated how inheritance is implemented in the context of an S3 class. It also provided a demonstration of how encapsulation is implemented under the framework of an S3 class.

One downside to the approach is that there is little type checking. It is possible to make changes to an object that can make it inconsistent with the original definition. When a change is made to an object, no checks are implemented to ensure that an object has the properties that are expected of it.

One way to avoid this issue is to make use of S4 classes. The approach associated with S4 classes is examined in the next chapter. Another advantage is that the S4 approach will look more familiar to those already familiar with object-oriented approaches to programming.

9
S4 Classes

This chapter is the third part in our introduction to programming. We examined s3 classes in the previous chapter. We will now examine s4 classes. The approach associated with s3 classes is more flexible, and the approach associated with s4 classes is a more formal and structured definition.

This chapter is roughly divided into four parts:

- **Class definition**: This section gives you an overview of how a class is defined and how the data (slots) associated with the class are specified

- **Class methods**: This section gives you an overview of how methods that are associated with a class are defined

- **Inheritance**: This section gives you an overview of how child classes that build on the definition of a parent class can be defined

- **Miscellaneous commands**: This section explains four commands that can be used to explore a given object or class

Introducing the Ant class

We defined the idea of control flow structures in *Chapter 7, Basic Programming*, and introduced the idea of an s3 class in *Chapter 8 ,S3 Classes*. We will now introduce the idea of s4 classes, which is a more formal way to implement classes in R. One of the odd quirks of s4 classes is that you first define the class along with its data, and then you define the methods separately.

As a result of this separation in the way a class is defined, we will first discuss the general idea of how to define a class and its data. We will then discuss how to add a method to an existing class. Next, we will discuss how inheritance is implemented. Finally, we will provide a few notes about other options that do not fit nicely in the categories mentioned earlier.

In the previous chapter, we took an example and then modified it. The approach associated with an S4 class is less flexible and requires a bit more forethought in terms of how a class is defined. We will take a different approach in this chapter and create a complete class from the beginning. In this case, we will build on an idea proposed by Cole and Cheshire. The authors proposed a cellular automata simulation to mimic how ants move within a colony.

As part of a simulation, we will assume that we need an Ant class. We will depart from the paper and assume that the ants are not homogeneous. We will then assume that there are male (drones) and female ants, and the females can be either workers or soldiers. We will need an ant base class, which is discussed in the first two sections of this chapter as a means to demonstrate how to create an S4 class. In the third section, we will define a hierarchy of classes based on the original Ant class. This hierarchy includes male and female classes. The worker class will then inherit from the female class, and the soldier class will inherit from the worker class.

Defining an S4 class

We will define the base Ant class called Ant. The class is represented in the following figure. The class is used to represent the fundamental aspects that we need to track for an ant, and we focus on creating the class and data. The methods are constructed in a separate step and are examined in the next section.

<<Base Class>> **Ant**
+Length: numeric(1) = 4mm +Position: numeric(3) = (0,0,0) +pA: numeric(1) = 0.05 +pl: numeric(1) = 0.1 +activityLevel: numeric(1) = 0.5
+SetLength(length: numeric(1)) +GetLength(): numeric (1) +SetPosition(currentPosition: numeric(3)) +GetPosition()(): numeric(3) +GetProbabilities(): numeric(2) +SetProbabilities(probabilities: numeric(2)) +SetActivityLevel(ants: Ant(N)) +SetActivityLevel(deactivate: logical) +GetActivityLevel(): numeric(1) +CalcSumDistances(ants : Ant (N)): numeric(1) +DetermineActivityLevel(ants: Ant(N))

A class is created using the setClass command. When creating the class, we specify the data in a character vector using the slots argument. The slots argument is a vector of character objects and represents the names of the data elements. These elements are often referred to as the slots within the class.

Some of the arguments that we will discuss here are optional, but it is a good practice to use them. In particular, we will specify a set of default values (the prototype) and a function to check whether the data is consistent (a validity function). Also, it is a good practice to keep all of the steps necessary to create a class within the same file. To that end, we assume that you will not be entering the commands from the command line. They are all found within a single file, so the formatting of the examples will reflect the lack of the R workspace markers.

The first step is to define the class using the setClass command. This command defines a new class by name, and it also returns a generator that can be used to construct an object for the new class. The first argument is the name of the class followed by the data to be included in the class. We will also include the default initial values and the definition of the function used to ensure that the data is consistent. The validity function can be set separately using the setValidity command. The data types for the slots are character values that match the names of the R data types which will be returned by the class command:

```
# Define the base Ant class.
Ant <- setClass(
    # Set the name of the class
    "Ant",

    # Name the data types (slots) that the class will track
    slots = c(
        Length="numeric",          # the length (size) of this ant.

        Position="numeric",         # the position of this ant.
                                    # (a 3 vector!)

        pA="numeric",               # Probability that an ant will
                                    # transition from active to
                                    # inactive.

        pI="numeric",               # Probability that an ant will
                                    # transition from inactive to
                                    # active.

        ActivityLevel="numeric"     # The ant's current activity
                                    # level.
```

```
    ),

# Set the default values for the slots. (optional)
prototype=list(
    Length=4.0,
    Position=c(0.0,0.0,0.0),
    pA=0.05,
    pI=0.1,
    ActivityLevel=0.5
    ),

# Make a function that can test to see if the data is consistent.
# (optional)
validity=function(object)
{
    # Check to see if the activity level and length is
    # non-negative.
    # See the discussion on the @ notation in the text below.
    if(object@ActivityLevel<0.0) {
        return("Error: The activity level is negative")
    } else if (object@Length<0.0) {
        return("Error: The length is negative")
    }
    return(TRUE)
}
)
```

With this definition, there are two ways to create an Ant object: one is using the new command and the other is using the Ant generator, which is created after the successful execution of the setClass command. Note that in the following examples, the default values can be overridden when a new object is created:

```
> ant1 <- new("Ant")
> ant1
An object of class "Ant"
Slot "Length":
[1] 4

Slot "Position":
[1] 0 0 0

Slot "pA":
[1] 0.05

Slot "pI":
```

```
[1] 0.1

Slot "ActivityLevel":
[1] 0.5
```

We can specify the default values when creating a new object.

```
> ant2 <- new("Ant",Length=4.5)
> ant2
An object of class "Ant"
Slot "Length":
[1] 4.5

Slot "Position":
[1] 0 0 0

Slot "pA":
[1] 0.05

Slot "pI":
[1] 0.1

Slot "ActivityLevel":
[1] 0.5
```

The object can also be created using the generator that is defined when creating the class using the setClass command.

```
> ant3 <- Ant(Length=5.0,Position=c(3.0,2.0,1.0))
> ant3
An object of class "Ant"
Slot "Length":
[1] 5

Slot "Position":
[1] 3 2 1

Slot "pA":
[1] 0.05

Slot "pI":
[1] 0.1

Slot "ActivityLevel":
[1] 0.5
```

```
> class(ant3)
[1] "Ant"
attr(,"package")
[1] ".GlobalEnv"
> getClass(ant3)
An object of class "Ant"
Slot "Length":
[1] 5

Slot "Position":
[1] 3 2 1

Slot "pA":
[1] 0.05

Slot "pI":
[1] 0.1

Slot "ActivityLevel":
[1] 0.5
```

When the object is created and a validity function is defined, the validity function will determine whether the given initial values are consistent:

```
> ant4 <- Ant(Length=-1.0,Position=c(3.0,2.0,1.0))
Error in validObject(.Object) :
   invalid class "Ant" object: Error: The length is negative
> ant4
Error: object 'ant4' not found
```

In the last steps, the attempted creation of ant4, an error message is displayed. The new variable, ant4, was not created. If you wish to test whether the object was created, you must be careful to ensure that the variable name used does not exist prior to the attempted creation of the new object. Also, the validity function is only executed when a request to create a new object is made. If you change the values of the data later, the validity function is not called.

Before we move on to discuss methods, we need to figure out how to get access to the data within an object. The syntax is different from other data structures, and we use @ to indicate that we want to access an element from within the object. This can be used to get a copy of the value or to set the value of an element:

```
> adomAnt <- Ant(Length=5.0,Position=c(-1.0,2.0,1.0))
> adomAnt@Length
[1] 5
```

```
> adomAnt@Position
[1] -1  2  1
> adomAnt@ActivityLevel = -5.0
> adomAnt@ActivityLevel
[1] -5
```

Note that in the preceding example, we set a value for the activity level that is not allowed according to the validity function. Since it was set after the object was created, no check is performed. The validity function is only executed during the creation of the object or if the validObject function is called.

One final note: it is generally a bad form to work directly with an element within an object, and a better practice is to create methods that obtain or change an individual element within an object. It is a best practice to be careful about the encapsulation of an object's slots. The R environment does not recognize the idea of private versus public data, and the onus is on the programmer to maintain discipline with respect to this important principle.

Defining methods for an S4 class

When a new class is defined, the data elements are defined, but the methods associated with the class are defined on a separate stage. Methods are implemented in a manner similar to the one used for S3 classes. A function is defined, and the way the function reacts depends on its arguments. If a method is used to change one of the data components of an object, then it must return a copy of the object, just as we saw with S3 classes.

The creation of new methods is discussed in two steps. We will first discuss how to define a method for a class where the method does not yet exist. Next, we will discuss some predefined methods that are available and how to extend them to accommodate a new class.

Defining new methods

The first step to create a new method is to reserve the name. Some functions are included by default, such as the initialize, print or show commands, and we will later see how to extend them. To reserve a new name, you must first use the setGeneric command. At the very least, you need to give this command the name of the function as a character string. As in the previous section, we will use more options as an attempt to practice safe programming.

The methods to be created are shown in preceding figure. There are a number of methods, but we will only define four here. All of the methods are accessors; they are used to either get or set values of the data components. We will only define the methods associated with the `length` slot in this text, and you can see the rest of the code in the examples available on the website. The other methods closely follow the code used for the `length` slot. There are two methods to set the activity level, and those codes are examined separately to provide an example of how a method can be overloaded.

First, we will define the methods to get and set the length. We will first create the method to get the length, as it is a little more straightforward. The first step is to tell R that a new function will be defined, and the name is reserved using the `setGeneric` command. The method that is called when an `Ant` object is passed to the command is defined using the `setMethod` command:

```
setGeneric(name="GetLength",
           def=function(antie)
           {
                  standardGeneric("GetLength")
           }
           )

setMethod(f="GetLength",
          signature="Ant",
          definition=function(antie)
          {
                  return(antie@Length)
          }
          )
```

Now that the `GetLength` function is defined, it can be used to get the length component for an `Ant` object:

```
>   ant2 <- new("Ant",Length=4.5)
> GetLength(ant2)
[1]  4.5
```

The method to set the length is similar, but there is one difference. The method must return a copy of the object passed to it, and it requires an additional argument:

```
setGeneric(name="SetLength",
           def=function(antie,newLength)
           {
                  standardGeneric("SetLength")
```

```
        }
    )

setMethod(f="SetLength",
        signature="Ant",
        definition=function(antie,newLength)
        {
            if(newLength>0.0) {
                antie@Length = newLength
            } else {
                warning("Error - invalid length passed");
            }

            return(antie)
        }
    )
```

When setting the length, the new object must be set using the object that is passed back from the function:

```
> ant2 <- new("Ant",Length=4.5)
> ant2@Length
[1] 4.5
> ant2 <- SetLength(ant2,6.25)
> ant2@Length
[1] 6.25
```

Polymorphism

The definition of s4 classes allows methods to be overloaded. That is, multiple functions that have the same name can be defined, and the function that is executed is determined by the arguments' types. We will now examine this idea in the context of defining the methods used to set the activity level in the Ant class.

Two or more functions can have the same name, but the types of the arguments passed to them differ. There are two methods to set the activity level. One takes a floating point number and sets the activity level based to the value passed to it. The other takes a logical value and sets the activity level to zero if the argument is FALSE; otherwise, it sets it to a default value.

The idea is to use the `signature` option in the `setMethod` command. It is set to a vector of class names, and the order of the class names is used to determine which function should be called for a given set of arguments. An important thing to note, though, is that the prototype defined in the `setGeneric` command defines the names of the arguments, and the argument names in both methods must be exactly the same and in the same order:

```
setGeneric(name="SetActivityLevel",
          def=function(antie,activity)
          {
                standardGeneric("SetActivityLevel")
          }
          )


setMethod(f="SetActivityLevel",
          signature=c("Ant","logical"),
          definition=function(antie,activity)
          {
              if(activity) {
                  antie@ActivityLevel = 0.1
              } else {
                  antie@ActivityLevel = 0.0
              }
              return(antie)
          }
          )


setMethod(f="SetActivityLevel",
          signature=c("Ant","numeric"),
          definition=function(antie,activity)
          {
              if(activity>=0.0) {
                  antie@ActivityLevel = activity
              } else {
                  warning("The activity level cannot be negative")
              }
              return(antie)
          }
          )
```

Once the two methods are defined, R will use the class names of the arguments to determine which function to call in a given context:

```
> ant2 <- SetActivityLevel(ant2,0.1)
> ant2@ActivityLevel
[1] 0.1
> ant2 <- SetActivityLevel(ant2,FALSE)
> ant2@ActivityLevel
[1] 0
```

There are two additional data types recognized by the `signature` option: `ANY` and `missing`. These can be used to match any data type or a missing value. Also note that we have left out the use of ellipses (…) for the arguments in the preceding examples. The ... argument must be the last argument and is used to indicate that any remaining parameters are passed as they appear in the original call to the function. Ellipses can make the use of the overloaded functions in a more flexible way than indicated. More information can be found using the `help(dotsMethods)` command.

Extending the existing methods

There are a number of generic functions defined in a basic R session, and we will examine how to extend an existing function. For example, the `show` command is a generic function whose behavior depends on the class name of the object passed to it. Since the function name is already reserved, the `setGeneric` command is not used to reserve the function name.

The `show` command is a standard example. The command takes an object and converts it to a character value to be displayed. The command defines how other commands print out and express an object. In the preceding example, a new class called `coordinate` is defined; this keeps track of two values, *x* and *y*, for a coordinate, and we will add one method to set the values of the coordinate:

```
# Define the base coordinates class.
Coordinate <- setClass(
    # Set the name of the class
    "Coordinate",

    # Name the data types (slots) that the class will track
    slots = c(
        x="numeric",   # the x position
        y="numeric"    # the y position
        ),

    # Set the default values for the slots. (optional)
```

```
    prototype=list(
        x=0.0,
        y=0.0
        ),

    # Make a function that can test to see if the data is consistent.
    # (optional)
    # This is not called if you have an initialize function defined!
    validity=function(object)
    {
        # Check to see if the coordinate is outside of a circle of
        # radius 100
        print("Checking the validity of the point")
        if(object@x*object@x+object@y*object@y>100.0*100.0) {
            return(paste("Error: The point is too far ",
            "away from the origin."))
        }
        return(TRUE)
    }
    )


# Add a method to set the value of a coordinate
setGeneric(name="SetPoint",
           def=function(coord,x,y)
           {
                standardGeneric("SetPoint")
           }
           )


setMethod(f="SetPoint",
          signature="Coordinate",
          def=function(coord,x,y)
          {
               print("Setting the point")
               coord@x = x
               coord@y = y
               return(coord)
          }
          )
```

We will now extend the show method so that it can properly react to a coordinate object. As it is reserved, we do not have to use the setGeneric command but can simply define it:

```
setMethod(f="show",
          signature="Coordinate",
          def=function(object)
          {
                  cat("The coordinate is X: ",object@x," Y:
          ",object@y,"\n")
          }
          )
```

As noted previously, the signature option must match the original definition of a function that you wish to extend. You can use the getMethod('show') command to examine the signature for the function. With the new method in place, the show command is used to convert a coordinate object to a string when it is printed:

```
> point <- Coordinate(x=1,y=5)
[1] "Checking the validity of the point"
> print(point)
The coordinate is X:  1  Y:  5
> point
The coordinate is X:  1  Y:  5
```

Another import predefined method is the initialize command. If the initialize command is created for a class, then it is called when a new object is created. That is, you can define an initialize function to act as a constructor. If an initialize function is defined for a class, the validator is not called. You have to manually call the validator using the validObject command. Also note that the prototype for the initialize command requires the name of the first argument to be an object, and the default values are given for the remaining arguments in case a new object is created without specifying any values for the slots:

```
setMethod(f="initialize",
          signature="Coordinate",
          def=function(.Object,x=0.0,y=0.0)
          {
                print("Checking the point")
                .Object = SetPoint(.Object,x,y)
                validObject(.Object) # you must explicitly call the
                                     # inspector
                return(.Object)
          }
          )
```

Now, when you create a new object, the new `initialize` function is called immediately:

```
> point <- Coordinate(x=2,y=3)
[1] "Checking the point"
[1] "Setting the point"
[1] "Checking the validity of the point"
> point
The coordinate is X:  2  Y:  3
```

Using the `initialize` and `validity` functions together can result in surprising code paths. This is especially true when inheriting from one class and calling the `initialize` function of a parent class from the child class. It is important to test codes to ensure that the code is executing in the order that you expect. Personally, I try to use either `validator` or `constructor`, but not both.

Inheritance

The `Ant` class discussed in the first section of this chapter provided an example of how to define a class and then define the methods associated with the class. We will now extend the class by creating new classes that inherit from the base class. The original `Ant` class is shown in the preceding figure, and now, we will propose four classes that inherit from the base class. Two new classes that inherit from `Ant` are the `Male` and `Female` classes. The `Worker` class inherits from the `Female` class, while the `Soldier` class inherits from the `Worker` class. The relationships are shown in the following figure. The code for all of the new classes is included in our example codes available at our website, but we will only focus on two of the new classes in the text to keep our discussion more focused.

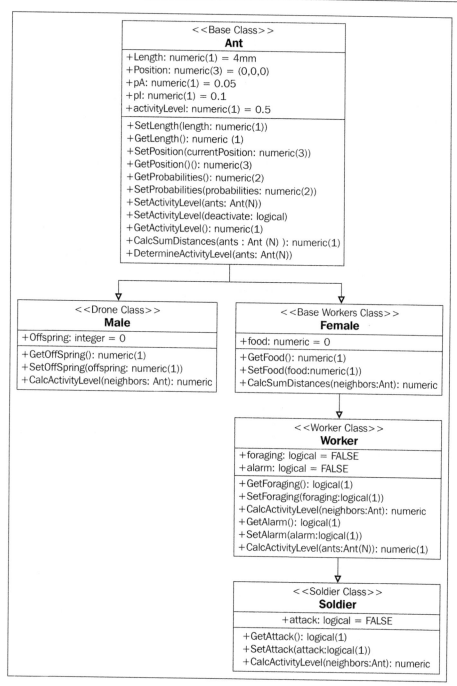

Relationships between the classes that inherit from the base Ant class

When a new class is created, it can inherit from an existing class by setting the `contains` parameter. This can be set to a vector of classes for multiple inheritance. However, we will focus on single inheritance here to avoid discussing the complications associated with determining how R finds a method when there are collisions. Assuming that the `Ant` base class given in the first section has already been defined in the current session, the child classes can be defined. The details for the two classes, `Female` and `Worker`, are discussed here.

First, the `FemaleAnt` class is defined. It adds a new slot, `Food`, and inherits from the `Ant` class. Before defining the `FemaleAnt` class, we add a caveat about the `Ant` class. The base `Ant` class should have been a virtual class. We would not ordinarily create an object of the `Ant` class. We did not make it a virtual class in order to simplify our introduction. We are wiser now and wish to demonstrate how to define a virtual class. The `FemaleAnt` class will be a virtual class to demonstrate the idea. We will make it a virtual class by including the VIRTUAL character string in the `contains` parameter, and it will not be possible to create an object of the `FemaleAnt` class:

```
# Define the female ant class.
FemaleAnt <- setClass(
    # Set the name of the class
    "FemaleAnt",

    # Name the data types (slots) that the class will track
    slots = c(
        Food ="numeric"      # The number of food units carried
        ),

    # Set the default values for the slots. (optional)
    prototype=list(
        Food=0
        ),

    # Make a function that can test to see if the data is consistent.
    # (optional)
    # This is not called if you have an initialize function defined!
    validity=function(object)
    {
        print("Validity: FemaleAnt")
        # Check to see if the number of offspring is non-negative.
        if(object@Food<0) {
            return("Error: The number of food units is negative")
        }
        return(TRUE)
```

```
    },

    # This class inherits from the Ant class
    contains=c("Ant","VIRTUAL")
    )
```

Now, we will define a WorkerAnt class that inherits from the FemaleAnt class:

```
# Define the worker  ant class.
WorkerAnt <- setClass(
    # Set the name of the class
    "WorkerAnt",

    # Name the data types (slots) that the class will track
    slots = c(
        Foraging ="logical",      # Whether or not the ant is actively
                                  # looking for food

        Alarm = "logical"         # Whether or not the ant is actively
                                  # announcing an alarm.

        ),

    # Set the default values for the slots. (optional)
    prototype=list(
        Foraging = FALSE,
        Alarm    = FALSE
        ),

    # Make a function that can test to see if the data is consistent.
    # (optional)
    # This is not called if you have an initialize function defined!
    validity=function(object)
    {
        print("Validity: WorkerAnt")
        return(TRUE)
    },

    # This class inherits from the FemaleAnt class
    contains="FemaleAnt"
    )
```

When a new worker is created, it inherits from the `FemaleAnt` class:

```
> worker <- WorkerAnt(Position=c(-1,3,5),Length=2.5)
> worker
An object of class "WorkerAnt"
Slot "Foraging":
[1] FALSE

Slot "Alarm":
[1] FALSE

Slot "Food":
[1] 0

Slot "Length":
[1] 2.5

Slot "Position":
[1] -1  3  5

Slot "pA":
[1] 0.05

Slot "pI":
[1] 0.1

Slot "ActivityLevel":
[1] 0.5

> worker <- SetLength(worker,3.5)
> GetLength(worker)
[1] 3.5
```

We have not defined the relevant methods in the preceding examples. The code is available in our set of examples, and we will not discuss most of it to keep this discussion more focused. We will examine the `initialize` method, though. The reason to do so is to explore the `callNextMethod` command. The `callNextMethod` command is used to request that R searches for and executes a method of the same name that is a member of a parent class.

We chose the initialize method because a common task is to build a chain of constructors that initialize the data associated for the class associated with each constructor. We have not yet created any of the initialize methods and start with the base Ant class:

```
setMethod(f="initialize",
          signature="Ant",
          def=function(.Object,Length=4,Position=c(0.0,0.0,0.0))
          {
               print("Ant initialize")
               .Object = SetLength(.Object,Length)
               .Object = SetPosition(.Object,Position)
               #validObject(.Object) # you must explicitly call the
                                     # inspector
               return(.Object)

          }
          )
```

The constructor takes three arguments: the object itself (.Object), the length, and the position of the ant, and default values are given in case none are provided when a new object is created. The validObject command is commented out. You should try uncommenting the line and create new objects to see whether the validator can in turn call the initialize method. Another important feature is that the initialize method returns a copy of the object.

The initialize command is created for the FemaleAnt class, and the arguments to the initialize command should be respected when the request to callNextMethod for the next function is made:

```
setMethod(f="initialize",
          signature="FemaleAnt",
          def=function(.Object,Length=4,Position=c(0.0,0.0,0.0))
          {
               print("FemaleAnt initialize ")
               .Object <- callNextMethod(.Object,Length,Position)
               #validObject(.Object)  # you must explicitly call the
     inspector
               return(.Object)
          }
          )
```

The callNextMethod command is used to call the initialize method associated with the Ant class. The arguments are arranged to match the definition of the Ant class, and it returns a new copy of the current object.

Finally, the initialize function for the `WorkerAnt` class is created. It also makes use of `callNextMethod` to ensure that the method of the same name associated with the parent class is also called:

```
setMethod(f="initialize",
          signature="WorkerAnt",
          def=function(.Object,Length=4,Position=c(0.0,0.0,0.0))
          {
              print("WorkerAnt initialize")
              .Object <- callNextMethod(.Object,Length,Position)
              #validObject(.Object) # you must explicitly call the
                                    #     inspector
              return(.Object)
          }
          )
```

Now, when a new object of the `WorkerAnt` class is created, the `initialize` method associated with the `WorkerAnt` class is called, and each associated method for each parent class is called in turn:

```
> worker <- WorkerAnt(Position=c(-1,3,5),Length=2.5)
[1] "WorkerAnt initialize"
[1] "FemaleAnt initialize "
[1] "Ant initialize"
```

Miscellaneous notes

In the previous sections, we discussed how to create a new class as well as how to define a hierarchy of classes. We will now discuss four commands that are helpful when working with classes: the `slotNames`, `getSlots`, `getClass`, and `slot` commands. Each command is briefly discussed in turn, and it is assumed that the `Ant`, `FemaleAnt`, and `WorkerAnt` classes that are given in the previous section are defined in the current workspace.

The first command, the `slotnames` command, is used to list the data components of an object of some class. It returns the names of each component as a vector of characters:

```
> worker <- WorkerAnt(Position=c(1,2,3),Length=5.6)
> slotNames(worker)
[1] "Foraging"    "Alarm"    "Food"    "Length"
[5] "Position"    "pA"       "pI"      "ActivityLevel"
```

The `getSlots` command is similar to the `slotNames` command. The difference is that the argument is a character variable which is the name of the class you want to investigate:

```
> getSlots("WorkerAnt")
       Foraging            Alarm            Food          Length        Position
      "logical"        "logical"       "numeric"       "numeric"       "numeric"
             pA          pI ActivityLevel
      "numeric"        "numeric"       "numeric"
```

The `getClass` command has two forms. If the argument is an object, the command will print out the details for the object. If the argument is a character string, then it will print out the details for the class whose name is the same as the argument:

```
> worker <- WorkerAnt(Position=c(1,2,3),Length=5.6)
> getClass(worker)
An object of class "WorkerAnt"
Slot "Foraging":
[1] FALSE

Slot "Alarm":
[1] FALSE

Slot "Food":
[1] 0

Slot "Length":
[1] 5.6

Slot "Position":
[1] 1 2 3

Slot "pA":
[1] 0.05

Slot "pI":
[1] 0.1

Slot "ActivityLevel":
[1] 0.5

> getClass("WorkerAnt")
Class "WorkerAnt" [in ".GlobalEnv"]
```

```
Slots:
```

Name: Position	Foraging	Alarm	Food	Length
Class: numeric	logical	logical	numeric	numeric

Name:	pA	pI	ActivityLevel
Class:	numeric	numeric	numeric

```
Extends:
Class "FemaleAnt", directly
Class "Ant", by class "FemaleAnt", distance 2
```

```
Known Subclasses: "SoldierAnt"
```

Finally, we will examine the slot command. The slot command is used to retrieve the value of a slot for a given object based on the name of the slot:

```
> worker <- WorkerAnt(Position=c(1,2,3),Length=5.6)
> slot(worker,"Position")
[1] 1 2 3
```

Summary

We introduced the idea of an S4 class and provided several examples. The S4 class is constructed in at least two stages. The first stage is to define the name of the class and the associated data components. The methods associated with the class are then defined in a separate step.

In addition to defining a class and its method, the idea of inheritance was explored. A partial example was given in this chapter; it built on a base class defined in the first section of the chapter. Additionally, the method to call-associated methods in parent classes was also explored, and the example made use of the constructor (or initialize method) to demonstrate how to build a chain of constructors.

Finally, four useful commands were explained. The four commands offered different ways to get information about a class or about an object of a given class.

For more information, you can refer to *Mobile Cellular Automata Models of Ant Behavior: Movement Activity of Leptothorax allardycei*, Blaine J. Cole and David Cheshire, *The American Naturalist*.

10
Case Study – Course Grades

This chapter is our first case study. We bring together the ideas from the previous chapters and provide an extended example. Some new ideas are introduced, and they should make more sense in the context of a full example.

This chapter is roughly divided into four parts:

- **The Course class**: This section gives you an overview of the S4 class that will contain a list of grades for a course. The grades are kept in a list with each graded task as a separate object.

- **The assignment classes**: This section gives you an overview of the S4 classes used to keep the grades for a specific graded task. This class has two derived classes. One derived class is to keep track of grades that have a numeric score, and the other is to keep track of grades that consist of letters.

- **Extending existing functions**: This section includes a brief discussion of how existing functions can be extended to react in an appropriate way to an object that is one of the assignment classes. We focus on the summary, plot, and show commands.

- **Extending operations**: This section includes a discussion on how to extend arithmetic and access functions by building on existing methods.

Overview

All the previous chapters focus on specific topics, and here we bring together a number of different topics to examine an extended example. All of the classes examined here are S4 classes. These classes are used to read in a CSV file that contains the grades for students in a class. There is one class that defines how to read a grade file and how to interpret a column. Another set of classes is defined and the classes are used to track the information for a single assignment. An object of this class will include all the scores for the assignments of all students.

We first discuss the new `Course` class, which is used to keep track of all the assignments. Next, we discuss the assignment classes that are used to keep track of the grades for a single assignment. Once the classes are defined, the details on extending the `summary`, `plot`, and `show` commands are given to demonstrate how common commands can be extended to react when passed a newly defined object. Finally, some basic arithmetic and accessor operators are redefined so that the R system will react in an appropriate manner when using familiar operations, such as addition or multiplication.

The `Course` class includes objects whose type is one of the assignment classes, and it seems more natural to define the assignment classes first. The actions of the assignment classes are more intricate and include more details, while the `Course` class is relatively straightforward. To keep the introduction to the classes more gentle, we'll first discuss the `Course` class.

The Course class

The `Course` class is used to keep track of all of the grades for a course. This class will read in the information from a file, decide whether grades are numeric grades or letter grades, and create an appropriate assignment object to hold the grades. The details for the class are shown in the following figure. We'll first discuss the data and then the methods associated with the class. We'll then give some details on how to define the class. Most of the code associated with the accessors is omitted for the sake of brevity, but the full code is available on the website associated with this book.

Course
+GradesFile: character()
+GradeTypes: character()
+Grades: list
+GetFileName(): character()
+SetFileName(course: Course,fileName: Character): character()
+GetGrades(): list
+SetGrades(course: Course,grades: list)
+GetGradeTypes(): character()
+SetGradeTypes(course: Course,gradeTypes: character())
+ReadGrades()

First, there are three data structures (slots) associated with the class. The first is the name of the CSV file that contains all of the grades for the class. The second is a vector of prefixes used to determine what kind of graded tasks are in the file. The last is a list that contains all of the assignments.

There are seven methods. All but one are used to set and get the values for the three slots. The accessor routines to get and set the filename are given here, and the others are not included in the text here. The last routine is used to read the grades, and it is a complex method that reads the data from the file and then determines whether the assignment has numerical or letter grades. It then defines an appropriate assignment object.

The definition of the Course class

The Course class definition is given and then the accessors for the slots are stated. It is an S4 class. In this case, we do not provide any checks to ensure that the information in the slots is consistent to reduce the complexity of the example:

```
###################################################
# Create the Course class to keep track of all grades
Course <- setClass(
    # Set the name for the class
    "Course",

    # Define the slots
    slots = c(
        GradesFile = "character",
        GradeTypes = "character",
        Grades     = "list"
        ),

    # Set the default values for the slots. (optional)
    prototype=list(
        GradesFile = "",
        GradeTypes = c("test","hw","quiz","project"),
        Grades     = list()
        ),

    # Make a function that can test to see if the data is consistent.
    # This is not called if you have an initialize function defined!
    validity=function(object)
    {
        return(TRUE)
    }
    )
```

Each of the slots includes a set of accessor functions to assist in retrieving or setting information tracked by the class. We only provide the details for one set of accessors. The methods to set and get the filename are given. Neither of these methods exist in the default R environment so they must be created first, as follows:

```
# Define the methods used to retrieve or set the values within a
Course object.
setGeneric(name="GetFileName",
           def=function(course)
           {
                standardGeneric("GetFileName")
           }
           )


setMethod(f="GetFileName",
          signature="Course",
          definition=function(course)
          {
               return(course@GradesFile)
          }
          )


setGeneric(name="SetFileName",
           def=function(course,fileName)
           {
                standardGeneric("SetFileName")
           }
           )


setMethod(f="SetFileName",
          signature="Course",
          definition=function(course,fileName)
          {
               course@GradesFile = fileName
               return(course)
          }
          )
```

Reading grades from a file

The last method examined is the method to read the data from a given file. We will examine the `Grades` list within the `Course` class before providing a listing. This slot is a list, and each element within the list is an assignment object. (The assignment classes are discussed in the next section of this chapter.) The name of the object within the list is the same as the name found in the first row of the CSV file.

The `ReadGrades` method first reads the `csv` file. It then goes through the columns that were read from the file, and the names of the columns are assumed to be in the first row of the file. If the first letters in the name of a column match one of the strings that are in the vector (found in the `GradeTypes` slot), then it is assumed that the column represents a graded item. There are two kinds of assignments: numerical grades or letter grades. If a column from the data file is determined to be a graded item, then its type is checked. If the type is a numeric type, then it is assumed that the course type is for a numeric grade (an object from the `NumericGrade` class); otherwise, it is assumed to be a letter grade (an object from the `LetterGrade` class):

```
setGeneric(name="ReadGrades",
        def=function(course)
        {
            standardGeneric("ReadGrades")
        }
        )


setMethod(f="ReadGrades",
        signature="Course",
        definition=function(course)
        {
            grades <- read.csv(GetFileName(course))
            convertedGrades <- list()
            courseTypes <- GetGradeTypes(course)
            for (gradeItem in names(grades))
            {
                # Go through each column from the file.
                for (type in courseTypes)
                {
                    # go through each course type and determine if
                    # this column is a quiz/test/hw/?
                    if(length(grep(type,gradeItem))>0)
                        {
                            # The prefix for the name matches one of
                            # the predefined types.
```

```
                                    if((class(grades[[gradeItem]])=="numer
   ic") ||

                                       (class(grades[[gradeItem]])=="integ
   er")) {

                                       thisItem <- NumericGrade()
                                       #print(paste("This item,",gradeItem,
                                       #   ",is a numeric grade item.",
                                       #   class(thisItem)))

         } else {
            thisItem <- LetterGrade()
            #print(paste("This item,",gradeItem,
            #      ", is a letter grade.",
            #      class(thisItem)))
         }
         # Convert the values into their
         # respective grades.
         thisItem <- SetValue(thisItem,
                 grades[[gradeItem]])
                                  #print(paste("class: ",class(thisItem)))
                                  convertedGrades[gradeItem] <- thisItem
                           }
                     }
                  }
               return(SetGrades(course,convertedGrades))
         }
         )
```

The `Course` class is used to organize the grades for a whole class. The scores for an individual assignment are kept in one of the assignment classes, which is examined in the following section.

The assignment classes

There are two assignment classes, and they are both derived from the assignment class. The first class is the `NumericGrade` class, which keeps track of a numeric grade. The second class is the `LetterGrade` class, which keeps track of a letter grade. The details of the classes are shown in the next figure. The definition of the `Assignment` class is given in the following figure, and the details about the accessors are omitted for the sake of brevity. The complete code is available on the website for this book.

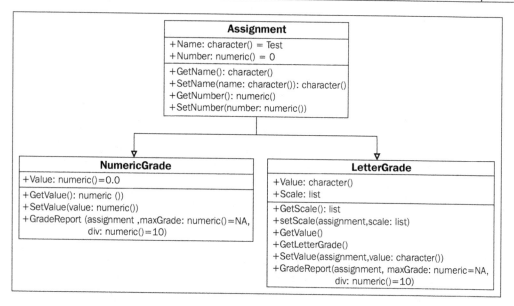

The details of the `NumericGrade` and `LetterGrade` classes are given in separate subsections in this chapter. Once the classes are given, examples are provided to demonstrate how to use the `Course` class to read the grades from a file and create the necessary assignment objects.

The assignment class is the base class for the `NumericGrade` and `LetterGrade` classes. The class only has two slots: the name and a number. The name is used to display the information related to the assignment, and the number can further identify the set of grades. For example, the grades for test 3 from a class might have a name, *Test*, and number set to the value of 3.

The definition for the class is given here:

```
#################################################
# Create the base assignment class
#
# This is used to represent the grades for one assignment.
Assignment <- setClass(
    # Set the name for the class
    "Assignment",

    # Define the slots
    slots = c(
        Name = "character",
```

```
        Number = "numeric"
        ),

    # Set the default values for the slots. (optional)
    prototype=list(
        Name = "Test",
        Number = as.integer(1)
        ),

    # Make a function that can test to see if the data is consistent.
    # This is not called if you have an initialize function defined!
    validity=function(object)
    {
        if(object@Number < 0) {
            object@Number <- 0
            warning(paste("A negative number for the assignment ",
            "number is passed. It is set to zero."))
        }
        return(TRUE)
    }
)
```

The primary purpose of the Assignment class is to act as the base class for other types of assignments. The two classes, NumericGrade and LetterGrade, that inherit from the assignment class are discussed in the following sections.

The NumericGrade class

The first class we examine that inherits from the Assignment class is the NumericGrade class. This class is used to retain the grades for an assignment whose grades are numbers. The class has only one slot, a numeric vector of grades. The definition is given here:

```
###############################################
# Create the class to keep track of the grades that are numeric in
# nature.
#
# This is used to represent the numeric grades for one assignment.
NumericGrade <- setClass(
    # Set the name for the class with a numeric grade associated with
    # it.
    "NumericGrade",

    # Define the slots
```

```
    slots = c(
        Value = "numeric"
        ),

    # Set the default values for the slots. (optional)
    prototype=list(
        Value = 0.0
        ),

    # Make a function that can test to see if the data is consistent.
    # (optional)
    # This is not called if you have an initialize function defined!
    validity=function(object)
    {
        if(object@Value < 0) {
            object@Value <- 0
            warning(paste("A negative number for the assignment value",
            "is passed. It is set to zero."))
        }
        return(TRUE)
    },

    # This class inherits from the Assignment class
    contains="Assignment"


    )
```

The methods for the class include the routines to set and get the values of the grades as well as a method to print out a report. The method to get the grades is given here as an example:

```
# Create the methods to retrieve and set the values of the
NumericGrade class.
setGeneric(name="GetValue",
          def=function(assignment)
          {
                standardGeneric("GetValue")
          }
          )

setMethod(f="GetValue",
          signature="NumericGrade",
          definition=function(assignment)
          {
```

```
                         return(assignment@Value)
            }
         )
```

There is one other method to be defined, and it is used to print out a report based on the scores. The method for the grade report prints out a five-point summary of the grades, the frequency of the grades divided into ten percent intervals (90-100 percent, 80-90 percent, 70-80 percent, and so on), a stem-leaf plot of the grades, and a sorted list of the grades. The `report` method includes a call to the summary command to get the five-point summary for the grades. The `summary` function is overridden, and the details are given in a later section, *Redefining existing functions*.

The definition of the report method is given here:

```
setGeneric(name="GradeReport",
           def=function(assignment,maxGrade=NA,div=10)
           {
                standardGeneric("GradeReport")
           }
         )


setMethod(f="GradeReport",
          signature="Assignment",
          definition=function(assignment,maxGrade=NA,div=10)
          {
               print(noquote(paste("Grade report for",
        GetName(assignment))))
print(noquote('')) 
print(summary(assignment))   # Print out a five
                             # point summary for the data
values <- GetValue(assignment)  # Get the raw scores.
if(is.na(maxGrade)) {
    # The maxGrade was not set. Assume the max score
    # from the data is the maximum possible.
    maxGrade <- max(values)
    warning(paste("The max gade is not set, and it is",
        "assumed to be",maxGrade))
                }

                skip <- maxGrade*div/100;              # Set
the width of the intervals.
```

```
        # Move the max grade up to make sure that the left sided
        # cut will have an interval to contain the top scores.
        while(maxGrade<=max(values))
            {
                maxGrade = maxGrade + skip
            }


        # Determine the number of intervals.
numLower <- ceiling((maxGrade-min(values))/skip)

# Determine all of the cutoff points
bins=c(seq(maxGrade-numLower*skip,
       max(c(values,maxGrade)),by=skip))

 # Convert the data  into factors
levs <- cut(values,breaks=bins,right=FALSE)

# Determine the frequencies for the  different levels.
gradeFreqs <- table(levs)

        print(noquote(''))
        print(noquote("Stem Leaf plot of grades:"))
        print(stem(values))
        print(noquote(''))

        print(noquote("Grade Frequencies:"))
        print(gradeFreqs)
        print(noquote(''))

        print(noquote("Sorted Grades:"))
        print(sort(values))
    }
    )
```

The LetterGrade class

The second class that inherits from the `Assignment` class is the `LetterGrade` class. This class is used to keep track of grades that are assigned as letter grades. It is similar to the `NumericGrade` class, except it has two slots. The first slot is a character vector with the grades. The second slot is a list that contains the possible letter grades as the name, and the value associated with each letter grade is its numeric value used for calculations.

The definition of the `LetterGrade` class is given here:

```
###############################################################
# Create the class to keep track of the grades that are letters in
# nature.
#
# This is used to represent the letter grades for one assignment.
LetterGrade <- setClass(
    # Set the name for the class with a numeric grade associated
    # with it.
    "LetterGrade",

    # Define the slots
    slots = c(
        Value = "character",
        Scale = "list"
        ),

    # Set the default values for the slots. (optional)
    prototype=list(
        Value = "F",
        Scale = list(
            'A+'=98,'A'=95,'A-'=92,
            'B+'=88,'B'=85,'B-'=83,
            'C+'=78,'C'=75,'C-'=73,
            'D+'=68,'D'=65,'D-'=63,
            'F+'=58,'F'=55,'F-'=53,
            "NA"=0)
        ),

    # Make a function that can test to see if the data is
    #consistent.
    # (optional)
    # This is not called if you have an initialize function
    #defined!
```

```
validity=function(object)
{
    pos <- grep(paste(object@Value,"$",sep=""),
        names(object@Scale))
    if(length(pos) != 1) {
        object@Value <- 'F-'
        warning("The grade is not recognized.")
    }
    return(TRUE)
},


    # This class inherits from the Assignment class
    contains="Assignment"


)
```

The class has the usual accessor methods to get and set the values of the slots. We give the method to set the value of the grades because it is a complex exercise. The method must convert each grade to a character because they may be passed as a factor. The method must also go through and make sure that each grade is the one that is already defined. It does this using the grep command and the names of the list in the Scales slot, as follows:

```
setMethod(f="SetValue",
        signature="LetterGrade",
        definition=function(assignment,value)
        {
            # Loop through each item in the vector of values. Also,
            # convert the value to a character vector. We need the
            # scale list inside the loop so grab a copy now for
            # later use.
            lupe <- 1
            value <- as.character(value)
            theScale <- GetScale(assignment)
            theNames <- names(theScale)
            while(lupe <= length(value))
                {
                # Determine whether this item can be found in the
                # list of scale items. Express it as a regular
                # expression and make sure it is an exact match
                # by using first and last place markers.
                thePattern <- paste("^",sub("\\+","\\\\+",
                    value[lupe]),"$",sep="")
                    pos <- grep(thePattern,theNames)
```

```
                    if(value[lupe]=="") {
                        #An empty string was passed.
                        value[lupe] <- "NA"
                    } else if(length(pos) != 1) {
        # This item was not found. Print a warning and make it an NA
                        warning(paste("The grade \"",value[lupe],
            "\"is not recognized. It is set to NA.",
        sep=""))
                            value[lupe] <- "NA"
                    }
                    lupe <- lupe + 1
                }
            assignment@Value <- value
            return(assignment)
        }
    )
```

The final method examined here is the method to print out a grade report. It is a simpler method compared to the same method in the NumericGrade class. In this case, the only results to print are the frequency of occurrences for each possible letter grade:

```
setMethod(f="GradeReport",
        signature="LetterGrade",
        definition=function(assignment,maxGrade=NA,div=10)
        {
            print(noquote(''))
            print(noquote(paste("Grade report for",
        GetName(assignment))))
    print(noquote(''))
    print(summary(assignment))   # Print out a five
                        # point summary for the data
        }
    )
```

Example – reading grades from a file

A short example is given to demonstrate how to read a class file. We assume that a CSV file, called shortList.csv, is in the current working directory. The first task to accomplish is to execute the file that contains the class definitions, grades.R. Once the class is defined, the filename is set, and the file is read.

First, in this example, the file with the `shortList.csv` grades is assumed to be the following:

```
section,test1,project1,final
3,75,B+,89
2,68,B,94
3,98,B+,110
2,76,A-,93
1,96,A+,112
1,81,B+,91
2,19,A,70
2,52,B+,70
2,88,A,71
```

The default value for the `GradeTypes` slot in the `Course` class is the following:

```
GradeTypes = c("test","hw","quiz","project")
```

Any column in the file whose name starts with one of the strings in the `GradeTypes` vector is assumed to be a recognized grade. The `test1`, `test2`, `hw1`, `hw2`, `hw3`, `quiz1`, `quiz2`, and `project1` columns are recognized as being a graded item. The column whose name is final is not in the default vector and is not recognized, so the `GradeTypes` slot should be replaced:

```
> source('grades.R')
> dir(pattern="csv$")
[1] "math100.csv"    "shortList.csv"
> course <- Course()
> course <- SetGradeTypes(course,c("test","hw","quiz","project",
                            "final"))
> course <- SetFileName(course,"shortList.csv")
> course <- ReadGrades(course)
> course
An object of class "Course"
Slot "GradesFile":
[1] "shortList.csv"

Slot "GradeTypes":
[1] "test"     "hw"         "quiz"      "project" "final"

Slot "Grades":
$test1
An object of class "NumericGrade"
```

```
Slot "Value":
[1] 75 68 98 76 96 81 19 52 88

Slot "Name":
[1] "Test"

Slot "Number":
[1] 1


$project1
An object of class "LetterGrade"
Slot "Value":
[1] "B+" "B"  "B+" "A-" "A+" "B+" "A"  "B+" "A"

Slot "Scale":
$'A+'
[1] 98

$A
[1] 95

$'A-'
[1] 92

$'B+'
[1] 88

$B
[1] 85

$'B-'
[1] 83

$'C+'
[1] 78

$C
[1] 75

$'C-'
[1] 73

$'D+'
```

```
[1] 68

$D
[1] 65

$'D-'
[1] 63

$'F+'
[1] 58

$F
[1] 55

$'F-'
[1] 53

$'NA'
[1] 0


Slot "Name":
[1] "Test"

Slot "Number":
[1] 1


$final
An object of class "NumericGrade"
Slot "Value":
[1]  89  94 110  93 112  91  70  70  71

Slot "Name":
[1] "Test"

Slot "Number":
[1] 1
```

Defining indexing operations

An object that is a `Course` class can have many assignment objects in its `Grades` slot. We did not define a special method to get a particular assignment, and no method is defined to save an assignment. We examine how to do this is in this section, and the discussion revolves around redefining the `[` operation.

First we redefine the `[` operation used to get an assignment. The idea is that we want to get a copy of an assignment by enclosing the name of the assignment as defined in the original file within square braces. To do this, we can redefine the operation. In this case, we want to be able to pass any kind of object within the braces, which will allow us to also use integers to index by location in the list:

```
setMethod("[",
          signature(x="Course",i="ANY"),
          definition=function(x,i=1)
          {
              #print(paste("Get grade item",i))
              return(x@Grades[[i]])
          }
          )
```

We would like to also be able to get a grade within an assignment. In this case, we will pass two arguments within the braces. The first task is to get the assignment using the previous definition and then get the grade within the assignment whose index matches the second argument:

```
setMethod("[",
          signature(x="Course",i="ANY",j="numeric"),
          definition=function(x,i=1,j=1)
          {
              #print(paste("course value",i,j))
              allGrades <- GetValue(x[i])
              return(allGrades[[j]])
          }
          )
```

We assume that the operations are defined in a file called `ops.R`. Once these methods are read and executed, the `[` operation is used in the following example to get a copy of `test1` or to examine the third grade in `test1`:

```
> source('grades.R')
> source('ops.R')
> source('overriding.R')
> course <- Course()
> course <- SetFileName(course,"shortList.csv")
```

```
> course <- ReadGrades(course)
> course['test1']
[1] Assignment: Test
[1] (9) Grades:
[1] 75 68 98 76 96 81 19 52 88
> course['test1',3]
[1] 98
>
```

The final topic to examine in this section is the use of the [operation to set the value of an entry. The approach is similar to the methods used to get information given earlier. The only difference is that instead of using the setMethod function, we use the setReplace method, and the last argument to the function is the value to set the corresponding entry in the appropriate object:

```
setReplaceMethod("[",
        signature("NumericGrade"),
        definition=function(x,i,value)
        {
            #print(paste("grade value",i,value))
            x@Value[i] = value
            return(x)
        }
        )

setReplaceMethod("[",
            signature("Course"),
            definition=function(x,i,j,value)
            {
                #print(paste("course grade",i,j,value))
                grades <- x@Grades[[i]]
                grades[j] <- value
                x@Grades[i] <- grades
                return(x)
            }
            )
```

With these definitions in place, a value within the course for a specific grade can be easily set, as follows:

```
> source('grades.R')
> source('ops.R')
> source('overriding.R')
>
> course <- Course()
```

```
> course <- SetFileName(course,"shortList.csv")
> course <- ReadGrades(course)
> print(course['test1'])
[1] Assignment: Test
[1] (9) Grades:
[1] 75 68 98 76 96 81 19 52 88
> print(course['test1',3])
[1] 98
>
> course['test1',3] <- 99.1
> print(course['test1',3])
[1] 99.1
>
```

Redefining existing functions

As mentioned previously, the summary, show, and plot commands are extended to react in an appropriate way when passed a NumericGrade or LetterGrade object. Extending these functions is done by simply defining a new method for these functions using the setMethod command. Each of these commands already exist, so it is not necessary to reserve the names using the setGeneric command. That is, we simply define the method to associate with the command when passed an object that is a member of the NumericGrade or LetterGrade class.

We extend the summary command in the first example. In this case, the function should have a different behavior if the object passed to it is NumericGrade versus LetterGrade. For an object that is LetterGrade, the summary command retrieves the grades and prints out a frequency table for the grades:

```
setMethod(f="summary",
          signature="LetterGrade",
          definition=function(object,...)
          {
              # Get the letter grades as factors and return the
              # frequency table.
              values <- GetLetterGrade(object)
              return(summary(as.factor(values)))
          }
          )
```

In this example, the only other kind of assignment that can be created is
`NumericGrade`, but in the future, the class may be extended. Instead of creating a
`summary` function solely for the `NumericGrade` class, we create a `summary` function
for its base class, `Assignment`. In this way, an argument to the `summary` command
that is derived from the `Assignment` class will obtain the object's grades, and the
grades are assumed to be a numeric vector. The `summary` command can then be
invoked on the vector:

```
setMethod(f="summary",
          signature="Assignment",
          definition=function(object,...)
          {
              # Get the grade values and return the five point
              # summary.
              values <- GetValue(object)
              return(summary(values))
          }
          )
```

In the following example, the necessary files are read, and the information from
the `shortList.csv` file is read. Copies of two different assignments, `test1` and
`project1`, are found, and a summary for each object is printed:

```
> source('grades.R')
> source('ops.R')
> source('overriding.R')
Creating a generic function for 'plot' from package 'graphics' in the
global environment
Creating a generic function for 'summary' from package 'base' in the
global environment
>
> course <- Course()
> course <- SetFileName(course,"shortList.csv")
> course <- ReadGrades(course)
> x <- course['test1']
> summary(x)
   Min. 1st Qu.  Median    Mean 3rd Qu.    Max.
  19.00   68.00   76.00   72.56   88.00   98.00
> p <- course['project1']
> summary(p)
 A A+ A-  B B+
 2  1  1  1  4
>
```

The files available in the repository for this book contain definitions for the show, summary, and plot commands. We examine one more here. The plot command for a NumericGrade object is a bit more complicated than the other examples. The plot command obtains the grades from the object passed to it, and it prints out a histogram, adds a box plot at the top of the histogram, and the rug command is used to display the data values on the same plot.

The arguments to the command include the maximum grade for the assignment. This argument is required because in some circumstances, extra credit is available and some students may achieve a higher score than is allocated for the rest of the class, and in other situations, no student may achieve a perfect score. If this argument is not provided, then the maximum score is used.

A second argument is included that indicates what percentages to use. The default is 10, which indicates that the breaks in the histogram are made at the 10 percent marks for the scores. For example, if the default of 10 is used, then the scores in the 90-100 range are counted together.

The final argument is the ellipses symbol (...), which indicates that other arguments can be passed to the function. The same symbol is used in the plot command within the method. The idea is that all of the extra parameters are passed to the plot command. This allows us to set a wide array of plot parameters through the method without having to catch any special cases:

```
setMethod(f="plot",
          signature="Assignment",
          definition=function(x,maxGrade=NA,div=10,...)
          {

              #print("Plotting an assignment")

              values <- GetValue(x) # Get the raw scores
              if(is.na(maxGrade)) {
                  # The maxGrade was not set. Assume the max score from
                  # the data is the maximum possible.
                  maxGrade <- max(values)
                  warning(paste("The max gade is not set, ",
                  " and it is assumed to be",
                  maxGrade))
              }
```

```
            skip <- maxGrade*div/100; # Set the width of the
                         # intervals.
#   Determine the number of intervals.
numLower <- ceiling((maxGrade-min(values))/skip)

# Determine the cut off values between the bins in the
# histogram.
bins=c(seq(maxGrade-numLower*skip,
            max(c(values,maxGrade)),by=skip))
if(max(bins)<max(values)) {
    # The bins do not include the maximum value. Adjust
    # the bound on the upper most bin.
    bins[length(bins)] <- max(values);
}
# Convert the data into factors
levs <- cut(values,breaks=bins,right=FALSE)
# Determine the frequencies for the different levels.
gradeFreqs <- table(levs)
# Get the max frequency
top <- max(gradeFreqs)
# Plot the histogram.
hist(values,breaks=bins,
    freq=TRUE,
    ylim=c(0,top+1),axes=FALSE,
    col=grey((seq(length(bins)-1,1,by=-1)/
                (length(bins)-1))),
     right=FALSE,...)

# Add a box plot across the top
boxplot(values,horizontal=TRUE,at=top+0.5,add=TRUE,
        axes=FALSE)

            # Plot the raw data as a strip chart across the bottom
            rug(values)
```

```
# Turn on only the left and lower axes.
axis(side=1,at=bins)
axis(side=2,at=seq(0,top+1,by=1))


}
)
```

In the following example, a larger data file is read. The results from `test2` are plotted, and the method automatically generates the plot as described earlier:

```
> source('grades.R')
> source('ops.R')
> source('overriding.R')
>
> course <- Course()
> course <- SetFileName(course,"math100.csv")
> course <- ReadGrades(course)
>
> x <- course['test2']
> plot(x,maxGrade=100,main='Student Scores From Test 2')
Warning message:
In plot.histogram(r, freq = freq1, col = col, border = border, angle =
angle,  :
    the AREAS in the plot are wrong -- rather use 'freq = FALSE'

>
```

Note that a warning message is printed. The maximum grade is specified as 100, but there are some students in the class who achieved a 102 because of extra credit. The breaks in the histogram include the students who achieved a higher grade than the maximum grade in the top 10 percent, and that set of values has a different width than the others. The resulting plot is shown in the following screenshot:

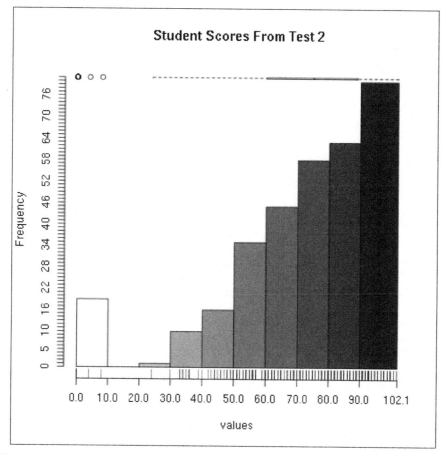

The histogram created by the plot command given the information in the math-100.csv grade file

Redefining arithmetic operations

The last topic that we're going to examine is how to define basic arithmetic operations on assignments. In particular, we'll examine how to perform arithmetic operations on two NumericGrade objects and how to add a set of values to a NumericGrade object. This can be done in the R environment by extending one of the sets of generic groups that is used to collect similar operations. The different groups include the Arith, Compare, Ops, Logic, Math, Math2, Summary, and Complex groups. The Ops group includes the Arith, Compare, and Logic operations, and we extend this group to include objects from the NumericGrades class.

We use the `setMethod` function for the `Ops` group to define operations involving `NumericGrade` objects. The resulting function obtains the grades and performs the requisite operation using the `callGeneric` command. The quirk of the system is that it must return a `NumericGrade` object, and the last step is to set the value of the grades for the first `NumericGrade` object sent to the function:

```
setMethod("Ops", signature(e1="NumericGrade", e2="NumericGrade"),
    function(e1, e2) {
        theSum <- callGeneric(GetValue(e1), GetValue(e2))
        return(SetValue(e1,theSum))
    }
)


setMethod("Ops", signature(e1="NumericGrade", e2="numeric"),
    function(e1, e2) {
        theSum <- callGeneric(GetValue(e1), e2)
        return(SetValue(e1,theSum))
    }
)


setMethod("Ops", signature(e1="numeric", e2="NumericGrade"),
    function(e1, e2) {
        theSum <- callGeneric(e1, GetValue(e2))
        return(SetValue(e1,theSum))
    }
)
```

In the following example, the grades from the `math100.csv` file are read. A copy of the scores taken from the `test1` and `test2` assignments are obtained, and the simple average is found by adding them and dividing by two:

```
> source('grades.R')
> source('ops.R')
> source('overriding.R')
>
> course <- Course()
> course <- SetFileName(course,"math100.csv")
> course <- ReadGrades(course)
> x <- course['test1']
> y <- course['test2']
> z <- (x + y)/2
> print(z)
[1] Assignment: Test
```

[1] (327) Grades:
 [1]   80.0   76.0   95.5   83.0   98.0   87.0   45.5   66.5   94.0   76.5
63.5   83.5
[13]   66.0   52.5   85.5   35.5   82.5   90.5   89.5   51.0   71.0   53.5
80.0   75.5
[25]   39.0   61.5   0.0   72.5   84.0   70.0   97.5   76.0   52.0   73.0
68.5   55.5
[37]   44.0   86.0   64.0   59.0   61.5   58.0   43.5   95.5   53.5   60.0
77.5   56.5
[49]   93.5   52.5   97.5   55.0   98.0   68.0   63.0   46.5   74.5   26.5
78.5   69.0
[61]   84.5   92.5   78.5   78.0   84.5   11.0   51.0   96.0   73.0   95.0
94.0   82.5
[73]   93.0   0.0   86.0   44.5   75.0   51.5   57.5 100.0   48.0   64.5
57.0   65.0
[85]   75.5   76.5   62.0   19.0   52.0   52.5   79.0   71.5   63.0   24.0
91.0   99.5
[97]   0.0   73.0   62.0   0.0   66.5   88.5   77.5   91.5   48.0   63.5
53.5   87.5
[109]   80.5   0.0   55.5   85.0   40.5   79.0   0.0   92.5   60.5   91.5
41.5   51.0
[121]   67.0   76.0   76.5   60.5   85.5   64.5   87.5   31.0   87.0   0.0
98.5   60.5
[133]   91.0   86.5   48.0   54.5   54.0   34.0   56.5   0.0   61.5   84.5
44.5   64.0
[145]   64.0   59.5   75.5   60.5   61.5   83.0   66.0   52.5   72.0   66.5
72.5   81.0
[157]   98.0   64.5   78.5   77.0   19.0   80.5   33.0   53.5   44.0   74.0
74.0   58.5
[169]   45.0   83.0   60.0   78.0   70.0   79.0   60.0   96.5   68.5   92.0
63.5   93.5
[181]   62.5   64.0   82.5   90.0   57.5   71.0   54.0   29.5   45.0   79.5
27.5   94.5
[193]   74.5   71.0   0.0   0.0   31.0   77.0   49.0   48.5   52.0 100.5
75.5   90.5
[205]   79.0   62.0   92.5   57.5   83.0   0.0   45.5   72.5   76.5   85.0
34.5   90.5
[217] 100.5   74.5   82.0   0.0   63.0   79.5   47.5   67.5   80.5   58.0
82.0   60.0
[229]   68.0   61.5   62.0   54.5   68.5   69.0   87.5   44.0   65.5   53.0
47.0   66.0
[241]   64.0   93.0   52.0   51.5   81.0   67.0   92.5   85.0   36.0   76.5
78.0   49.5
[253]   42.5   86.0   76.0   43.0   74.0   90.5   44.5   40.5   45.0   50.5
48.0   80.0
[265]   87.0   88.0   59.5   59.5   48.0   62.0   94.0   80.0   71.0   64.0
65.0   43.5

```
[277]   61.0    0.0   57.0   33.0   91.0  100.0   66.0   91.5   98.0   70.0
60.0   91.5
[289]   91.0   81.5   42.0   80.0   67.0   64.5   64.5   55.5   88.5   73.5
81.5   99.5
[301]   59.5   65.0   77.5   58.5   89.5  100.5   44.5   85.5    0.0   70.5
90.0   85.5
[313]   81.0   64.5   51.0   76.5   54.5   88.0   58.5   56.0   23.0   36.0
88.5   71.5
[325]   56.0   66.5   16.5
>
```

Summary

An extended example making use of S4 classes was examined in this chapter, and a set of classes are defined to read and track the grades for a class. The Course class keeps track of a number of assignments, and it reads the contents of a CSV file and automatically determines which columns are grades and whether or not they are numerical grades or letter grades.

The grades for a particular assignment are kept in one of two classes. The NumericGrade class keeps track of numerical grades, and the LetterGrade class keeps track of letter grades. Both classes are derived from the Assignment base class.

A number of examples were given, and highlights from the code were given. The full set of code can be found on the website associated with this book, and we recommend that you closely examine the code. The three files that include the definitions for this class are the grades.R, ops.R, and overriding.R files.

In the next chapter, another set of classes are developed. The classes in that chapter provide an example of a set of classes that can be used to generate the results from a stochastic process and manage the results from a large number of simulations. The classes can be used to generate results from either a discrete or continuous process, and the distribution of the results can be explored.

11

Case Study – Simulation

We will now examine a set of S3 classes designed to implement a Monte-Carlo simulation. The example scripts include a class to generate a single simulation as well as a class to run and collect the results from multiple simulations. The simulation class includes two derived classes. One is used for simulations of a discrete stochastic process, and the other is for simulations of a stochastic differential equation.

This section is roughly divided into the following parts:

- The simulation classes
- The Monte-Carlo class
- Examples

We will first examine a set of simulation classes that are designed to generate a single simulation of a stochastic system. The classes make use of a base class to manage the parameters. Two classes are derived from the base class. The first derived class is used to simulate a discrete stochastic system. The second derived class is used to approximate a stochastic differential equation.

After examining the simulation classes, a master class is used to manage the Monte-Carlo simulations. The Monte-Carlo class accepts a simulation class and collects the results from multiple simulations. Our focus is on the basic structure of the classes, so we do not discuss statistical methods for the data.

We briefly examine an example using the classes in the last section of this chapter. The example focuses on how to create an object from the discrete stochastic simulation class and how to generate results.

The simulation classes

The simulation classes consist of three parts. The `Simulation` class is the base class, and two classes, `DiscreteSimulation` and `ContinuousSimulation`, are derived from the base class. We assume that the definitions for these classes are kept in a separate file, `simulationS3.R`.

The base class, `Simulation`, is used to manage the parameters and results for a single simulation. The data includes the final time used in the simulation and accessor methods are defined for the data:

```
#######################Create the base simulation class
##
## This is used to represent a single simulation
Simulation <- function()
   {

      ## Create the list used to represent an
      ## object for this class
      me = list(
         simulationResults = matrix(0)
         )

      ## Set the name for the class
      class(me) <- append(class(me),"Simulation")
      return(me)


   }# Set the data values that are the result of a simulation.
setSimulation <- function(theSimulation)
    {
        UseMethod("setSimulation",theSimulation)
    }
setSimulation <- function(theSimulation,simulationResults)
    {
        ## Set the value of the  variable theSimulation
        theSimulation$simulationResults <- simulationResults
        return(theSimulation)
    }
]
## method to return the data from the current set of results.
getFinalValues <- function(theSimulation)
    {
        UseMethod("getFinalValues",theSimulation)
```

```
    }
getFinalValues <- function(theSimulation)
    {
        ## Get the value of the data pair at the last time step
        size <- dim(theSimulation$simulationResults)
        return(c(theSimulation$simulationResults[size[1],1],
                theSimulation$simulationResults[size[1],2]))
    }
```

Note that the class includes an addition method, getFinalValues, which is used to retrieve the last values approximated in the simulation. This method is required by the Monte-Carlo class defined in the next section. The results are used to determine the requisite statistics.

The next two classes are the DiscreteSimulation and ContinuousSimulation classes. The DiscreteSimulation class is used to generate an approximation to the discrete stochastic system given by the following equation:

$$x_{n+1} = ax_n + bx_n y_n + N_1 W_1, y_{n+1} = gx_n + dy_n + N_2 W_2$$

In the preceding equation, a, b, N1, g, d, and N2 are constants, and W1 and W2 are normally distributed random variables with a mean of zero and a standard deviation of one. The ContinuousSimulation class is used to generate an approximation using the Milstein scheme to the stochastic differential equation:

$$dx = (axy + by)dt + N_1 dW_1, dy = (gx + dy)dt + N_2 dW_2$$

In the preceding equation, a, b, N1, g, d, and N2 are constants, and W1 and W2 are independent Wiener processes.

The complete scripts for all of the classes can be found in the code that accompanies this text. In the interest of brevity, we only look at one derived class: the DiscreteSimulation class. The definition of the class is given here:

```
############################################################
## Create a simulation for a discrete simulation.
##
## This is used to represent the results from a discrete simulation.
DiscreteSimulation <- function()
    {
        ## Define the base class and get the environment
```

```
me <- Simulation()
me$N <- 0

## Set the name for the class with a numeric grade associated with
## it.
class(me) <- append(class(me),"DiscreteSimulation")
return(me)
}
```

The final method specific to this class is the `singleSimulation` method that is used to conduct one simulation and save the results. The methods necessary to define the discrete simulation class are as follows:

```
# the methods to do the actual simulations.
singleSimulation <- function(simulation,N,T,x0,y0,alpha,beta,
   gamma,delta, noiseOne,noiseTwo)
  {
    UseMethod("singleSimulation",simulation)
  }


singleSimulation.DiscreteSimulation <-function(
   simulation,N,T,x0,y0,alpha,beta,gamma,delta,noiseOne,noiseTwo)
  {
    ## Make an approximation for one run of the discrete model
    ## with the given parameters. Store the approximation in
    ## the simulation slot when done.

    ## initialize the necessary variables.
    x <- matrix(data=double(N*2),nrow=N,ncol=2)
    x[1,1] <- x0
    x[1,2] <- y0
    lupe <- 2

    ## Go through and make N iterations of the stochastic model.
    while(lupe <= N)
      {
        dW <- rnorm(2,mean=0,sd=1)      # Generate two random numbers
                                        # with a normal dist.
        ## Take one step of the discrete model
        x[lupe,1] <- alpha*x[lupe-1,1] + beta*x[lupe-1,1]*x[lupe-1,2]
+
          noiseOne*dW[1]
        x[lupe,2] <- gamma*x[lupe-1,1] + delta*x[lupe-1,2] +
          noiseTwo*dW[2]
```

```
        lupe <- lupe + 1
    }

    ## Save the simulation and return the result.
    simulation <- setSimulation(simulation,x)
    return(simulation)
}
```

The Monte-Carlo class

The final class examined is the MonteCarlo class. The MonteCarlo class is used to keep track of the results from multiple simulations. Here, we provide a partial list of the code for the class and then provide the methods used to generate multiple simulations.

First, the code required to define the class is given here:

```
###############################################################
# Create the Monte Carlo class
#
# This class is used to make many simulations
MonteCarlo <- function()
{

    # Define the slots
    me = list(

        ## First define the parameters for the stochastic model
        N        = 0,
        T        = 0,
        x0       = 0,
        y0       = 0,
        alpha    = 0,
        beta     = 0,
        gamma    = 0,
        delta    = 0,
        noiseOne = 0,
        noiseTwo = 0,

        ## Define the data to track and the number of trials
        xData = 0,
        yData = 0

    )
```

```
    ## Set the name for the class
    class(me) <- append(class(me),"MonteCarlo")
    return(me)
}


# Define the method used to initialize the data prior to a run.
prepare <- function(monteCarlo,number)
    {
        UseMethod("prepare",monteCarlo)
    }
prepare.MonteCarlo <- function(monteCarlo,number)
    {
        ## Set the number of trials and initialize the values to
        ## zeroes.
        monteCarlo$xData <- double(number)
        monteCarlo$yData <- double(number)
        return(monteCarlo)
    }
```

The class requires an additional method. The `simulations` method is used to create multiple simulations and record the results:

```
simulations <- function(monteCarlo,number,simulation)
  {
    UseMethod("simulations",monteCarlo)
  }


simulations.MonteCarlo <- function(monteCarlo,number,simulation)
  {
    ## Set the number of trials and initialize the values
    monteCarlo <- prepare(monteCarlo,number)
    params <- getParams(monteCarlo)    # get the parameters

    ## Perform the simulations
    lupe <- 0
    while(lupe < number)
      {
        lupe <- lupe + 1 # increment the count
        ## Perform a single simulation.
        simulation <- singleSimulation(
          simulation,
          params[1],params[2],params[3],params[4],params[5],
          params[6],params[7],params[8],params[9],params[10])
```

```
                  ## Get the last values of the simulation and record them.
                  values <- getFinalValues(simulation)
                  monteCarlo <- setValue(monteCarlo,values[1],values[2],lupe)
              }

           return(monteCarlo)
       }
```

Examples

We will now provide a brief example to demonstrate how to use the `Simulation` and `MonteCarlo` classes described in the previous sections. We focus on the discrete simulation class, but additional examples can be found in the code that accompanies this text. In this example, we assume that the definitions for the `simulation` and `MonteCarlo` classes are contained in two files, `simulationS3.R` and `monteCarloS3.R`.

The Monte-Carlo simulations can be created by first creating an object from the `MontyCarlo` class and setting the values of the parameters as follows:

```
> source('simulationS3.R')
> source('monteCarloS3.R')

> monty <- MonteCarlo()
> monty$setParams(100,1,
                  1.0,2.0,
                  1.2,-0.3,0.65,0.2,
                  0.03,0.04)
```

Now that an object from the `MonteCarlo` class is defined, an object from the `DiscreteSimulation` class is created, and the simulation object is used to generate the results from 500 simulations:

```
> a <- DiscreteSimulation()
> monty <- simulations(monty,500,a)
```

At this point, the `monty` object has the results from 500 simulations. The results can be found using the `getValues` method, as follows:

```
> summary(results[,1])
   Min. 1st Qu.  Median    Mean 3rd Qu.    Max.
 0.6480  0.7792  0.8231  0.8213  0.8595  1.0110
> summary(results[,2])
   Min. 1st Qu.  Median    Mean 3rd Qu.    Max.
 0.4978  0.6232  0.6590  0.6632  0.7064  0.8918
```

Alternatively, methods can be defined that extend existing methods. For example, the `hist` function can be extended to accommodate an object from the `MonteCarlo` class:

```
# the methods to plot the results
hist.MonteCarlo <- function(x,main="",...)
    {
        par(mfrow=c(2,1))
        values <- getValues(x)
        isValid <- (!is.na(values[,1])) && (!is.infinite(values[,1]))
        hist(values[isValid,1],xlab="x",main=main,...)
        hist(values[isValid,2],xlab="y",main="",...)
    }
```

With this definition, a histogram can be easily created:

```
hist(monty,main="Results from a Discrete Simulation")
```

Summary

An example of an `S3` class was defined that can be used to keep track of a set of simulations. The classes include a separate class used to create a single simulation. The single simulation can be an approximation of either a discrete or continuous stochastic process. Another class is developed that can keep track of the results from a large number of simulations.

In the next chapter, we look at another extended example. The focus in the next chapter is on creating a set of S3 classes to provide a general way to handle regression tasks for a variety of data types. You can download this chapter from `https://www.packtpub.com/sites/default/files/downloads/6682OS_Case_Study_Regression.pdf`.

Package Management

A brief overview of working with packages is provided here. This is given as a reference to the basic commands used to manage packages. It is not exhaustive and serves only as a brief reference to manage packages associated with your installation of R.

The appendix has four parts:

- An overview on how to access a package
- An overview on how to install a package
- An overview on how to remove a package
- An overview on how to update packages

One of R's greatest strengths is the ability to use specialized packages, and a wide range of packages are available. Some of the packages are included in the regular installation, and some packages must be installed and maintained separately. We provide a brief overview of how to install, remove, and upgrade the installed packages on your system.

We first discuss two commands that are commonly used when working with packages. The first is the `installed.packages` command. This command will list all of the packages that are part of your installation. The other command is the `library` command. The `library` command is used to tell R to make use of the commands available in a given library. In the following example, the first command displays information about the splines package, and the second command must be entered before using the spline package:

```
> library(help = "splines")
> library(splines)
```

If a package is not part of your installation, you need to install it. The command to install a package is, oddly enough, the install.package command. In the following example, the car package, which is used for additional regression options, is installed. The full details are not provided. You must reply to a series of questions posed and then R will automatically fetch and install the package for you:

```
> install.packages("car")
```

A package can also be easily removed using the remove.packages command. In the following example, we remove the car package:

```
> remove.packages("car")
```

The last topic discussed is how to update your packages. To update all of your packages, simply use the update.packages command. In the following example, the command is entered and the full details are not provided. After submitting the command, you are given a list of packages that can be updated and you must decide which packages will be updated on your system:

```
> update.packages()
```

Index

as function 20, 21
is function 20, 21
S_PLUS language 90
sprintf function 68
stop command 89
storage.mode command 10
strftime command 75
strings
  converting, to time data types 72-75
  splitting 67
  time data types, converting to 75
strptime command 72
strsplit command 67
sub command 70
substring
  changing 66
  extracting 66
  location 65

T

tables, data structure 27, 28
tapply command 35
time data types
  converting, to strings 75
  operations on 76, 77
  strings, converting to 72-75

transform case 67
TRUE value 13
typeof command 12

U

update.packages command 170
UseMethod command 99, 102

V

vectors, data structure 23, 24

W

warning command 89
while loop
  about 82, 83
  versus for loop 83
workspace
  about 9, 10
  saving 44
writeBin command 47
writeChar command 48
writeLines command 48

Thank you for buying
R Object-oriented Programming

About Packt Publishing

Packt, pronounced 'packed', published its first book "*Mastering phpMyAdmin for Effective MySQL Management*" in April 2004 and subsequently continued to specialize in publishing highly focused books on specific technologies and solutions.

Our books and publications share the experiences of your fellow IT professionals in adapting and customizing today's systems, applications, and frameworks. Our solution based books give you the knowledge and power to customize the software and technologies you're using to get the job done. Packt books are more specific and less general than the IT books you have seen in the past. Our unique business model allows us to bring you more focused information, giving you more of what you need to know, and less of what you don't.

Packt is a modern, yet unique publishing company, which focuses on producing quality, cutting-edge books for communities of developers, administrators, and newbies alike. For more information, please visit our website: www.packtpub.com.

About Packt Open Source

In 2010, Packt launched two new brands, Packt Open Source and Packt Enterprise, in order to continue its focus on specialization. This book is part of the Packt Open Source brand, home to books published on software built around Open Source licenses, and offering information to anybody from advanced developers to budding web designers. The Open Source brand also runs Packt's Open Source Royalty Scheme, by which Packt gives a royalty to each Open Source project about whose software a book is sold.

Writing for Packt

We welcome all inquiries from people who are interested in authoring. Book proposals should be sent to author@packtpub.com. If your book idea is still at an early stage and you would like to discuss it first before writing a formal book proposal, contact us; one of our commissioning editors will get in touch with you.

We're not just looking for published authors; if you have strong technical skills but no writing experience, our experienced editors can help you develop a writing career, or simply get some additional reward for your expertise.

SignalR Real-time Application Cookbook

ISBN: 978-1-78328-595-2   Paperback: 292 pages

Use SignalR to create real-time, bidirectional, and asynchronous applications based on standard web technologies

1. Build high performance real-time web applications.

2. Broadcast messages from the server to many clients simultaneously.

3. Implement complex and reactive architectures.

Data Manipulation with R

ISBN: 978-1-78328-109-1   Paperback: 102 pages

Perform group-wise data manipulation and deal with large datasets using R efficiently and effectively

1. Perform factor manipulation and string processing.

2. Learn group-wise data manipulation using plyr.

3. Handle large datasets, interact with database software, and manipulate data using sqldf.

Please check **www.PacktPub.com** for information on our titles